Roxanne is a now-retired teacher who experienced a side of Iran that most people never see. She describes her life as it intersects with the Middle East during some of the most turbulent times in the Iran-Iraq war. She met and married an Iranian man only one month before the Iranian hostage crisis in America, lived in Iran from 1984 to 1988 during the war, and witnessed firsthand the aftermath of several bombings. Her husband developed cancer and died in the most famous mosque in Iran, hours after their ninth anniversary, and experienced one of the largest funeral processions for a civilian. This is the true story of the life and experiences she had living there.

This book is dedicated to the pillars in my life.

To my Iranian family, with help from my son, Alex, and most importantly, my dearest daughter, Angela.

May this book keep the memory of your father alive.

R.E. Daniel

JUST ADD ROSE WATER

Adventures of an American in Iran

AUSTIN MACAULEY PUBLISHERS™

LONDON • CAMBRIDGE • NEW YORK • SHARJAH

Ordering Information
Quantity sales: Special discounts are available on quantity purchases by corporations, associations, and others. For details, contact the publisher at the address below.

Publisher's Cataloging-in-Publication data
Daniel, R.E.
Just add Rose Water

ISBN 9798886932263 (Paperback)
ISBN 9798886932270 (ePub e-book)

Library of Congress Control Number: 2023921556

www.austinmacauley.com/us

First Published 2024
Austin Macauley Publishers LLC
40 Wall Street, 33rd Floor, Suite 3302
New York, NY 10005
USA

mail-usa@austinmacauley.com
+1 (646) 5125767

Table of Contents

1

Ends and Beginnings

Setting: Kashan, Iran – September 10, 1988

I am surrounded on all sides by women clothed in somber black veils. I can barely see their faces, but I know that they are crying. I am leading all of these women down the street, but following in the footsteps of hundreds of men. A dusty bleak street stretches under our feet as we march forward. Morning has just begun, and I have not yet felt the heat of the sun. The speakers are blaring in the distance, and the man with the microphone is chanting to the crowd, and they respond in unison. Men are beating their chests and echoing the chants. An eerie feeling is left in my gut, knowing that this hardship is almost over. My husband is being held aloft in the air by a myriad of men, as tears streak down their faces. My brother-in-law and male family members are following directly behind my

9

husband. People on the sides of the street watch with solemn dignity. They watch me with careful curiosity, to discern how a foreigner reacts to an Iranian funeral.

Let me turn back the sands of time to the beginning and explain how I got myself here. It has taken me over 30 years to write this story. I hope that you will understand that what I am about to tell you is all true to the best of my memories. Luckily, I have pictures to back up what I am writing and to give evidence of the amazing life I have had. I have gone through a war, scary creatures like sun spiders running over my feet, snakes in my bathroom, love, and death, but I am still thriving. As my father said many times about me, I could go through hell and a load of shit, and I will still come out smelling like a rose. To those others who decide to join me on my ten-year journey, I am telling this story for my daughter. I have written this part of my life over and over again in my dreams. I have given much thought to what words I should say, it is time to buckle down and tell you a story. Although I have to laugh at myself. If this story ever got made into a movie, I have always wanted Drew Barrymore to play my character.

My father was in the Army so I considered myself to be a military brat, never staying in one place too long. I had one older brother and an adopted brother from Germany. I was born in New Jersey, lived in Washington State as a baby, then moved to New Mexico and El Paso, Texas for my first years in school. My mother, being from Georgia, moved my siblings and I back there once my parents got divorced. I would bounce around from state to state over the course of my adolescence but my mother always delivered us back to Georgia where I have lived for a substantial part of my life.

Growing up, I listened to John Denver, Jim Croce, James Taylor, and other musicians of the 1970s. I witnessed the different political movements in this era, such as the Equal Rights Amendment and demonstrations against the war in Vietnam, in which I lost my brother Butch. I was active in the Mormon church that my grandparents belonged to but also went with an aunt to the Salvation Army church. I was open to seeing things from different people's viewpoints. As a little girl, being taught to be seen and not heard, my observations of life helped me learn to be self-sufficient. My mother used to brag about how my brothers and I were always well behaved and quiet. She threatened to put the fear of God into us if we were noisy. That's why when I look at the world, I am rarely surprised by the things that I see.

Many things affected me, like the movie *Lawrence of*

Arabia. I remember the actor Peter O'Toole being gifted his Arabic clothes for the first time. He got out into the desert and started dancing around with his Agal (Headdress). I imagined myself in that situation. How strange it must have felt to be in a completely new environment and have to understand a different culture and language.

I'm also a product of many things I read when I was young. My favorite books were *Caravans* and *The Source* by James Michener. These stories would take me to those alien places before I even thought about marrying somebody from an area like that. It felt like destiny for me to end up in the middle east. I really wasn't looking for somebody from there but it just happened.

I didn't start this book to say that I have any set of political beliefs, or that I am against America. No, I love America. I love the country I live in, but I do love to explore the world. We are not just one culture. Being part of two different cultures helped me see, that while we have different beliefs around the world, we are more alike than we realize. Although I am truly All-American, I have a very special connection to a loving family in Iran, by my dear daughter Angela. As the saying goes, we are all separated by six degrees of Kevin Bacon.

Life is full of wonders and for about 10 years I had a serendipitous life. I didn't plan it, I found it by accident. When my white picket fence door closed, an intricate archaic door opened, and I ran through it! My curiosity encouraged me to continue even though it was not a straight path. It was more like a labyrinth.

Some of the major locations mentioned in the story are as follows. In the United states, we have Columbus and Atlanta, Georgia. And in Iran we have Natanz, Isfahan, Shiraz, Tehran, Yazd, Mashhad, Qom, and Kashan. Let me begin to tell you about this remarkable part of my life. First, let me explain the main characters in my story. Although some names have been changed to protect those still alive, all the stories remain true.

Hossein Atrchin-Kashi – my husband (Now deceased). He was seven years older than me. I meet him when I was about 20, and married him when I was 23. He was a bodybuilder and had his bachelor's, master's, and doctorate degrees in Business.

Shirin – Hossein's sister, and my sister-in-law (Currently alive and in Iran). She used to work as a principal for an elementary school in Tehran, but is now retired. She was older than my husband by about five years. She speaks no English except for a few words.

Mohammad – Hossein's brother, and my brother-in-law (Now deceased). He was at least seven years older than my husband and was a civil engineer. He had a private business, but also worked for the government. He was fluent in English.

Ava – Mohammad's wife, and my sister-in-law (Currently alive and in Iran). She has a nursing degree and used to teach nursing at a university, but is now retired. She is about five years older than me. She speaks English fluently just like her husband did.

Along with me, there were a slew of people who take minor roles in my story. There were dozens of my husband's extended family members, almost like everybody in town was related to him in some way. Unlike America, where we tend to move around a lot, these people stayed local for upwards of hundreds, maybe even thousands of years. They had an ancient history unlike anything I've ever seen.

2
Coming to Iran

I had always been interested in different parts of the world. Being from a military family I was used to going to different schools. Between Connecticut, Texas, and then finally Georgia for my final school years, I experienced almost a new school every year.

Having attended Columbus College in Columbus, Georgia in the fall of 1974, was where I met my lifelong friend Hilda. She was of mixed heritage, and was half German and half Puerto Rican decent. We had a delegation of Iranian students at our small college too, that greatly interested me. Never had I met someone from that country before. Being an avid reader and having read many novels about the Middle East made me curious about the region. I had always loved the dry desert areas of New Mexico and West Texas in America and had a fondness for this type of environment. I can still remember standing near our old station wagon and peering over a map my father had laid out for us. He showed me how the roads would connect around the desert and would tell me how to survive if I ever got lost. "Don't panic," he would say. "Think of what you need to do to survive." Then we would stay late into the evening and watch the stars come out. The Milky Way was very intriguing to me along with the different plants and creatures in the desert. Parts of the Middle East were similar to these states.

Being part of a group of international students, including Iranians, was a lot of fun. Some of the Iranian guys cooked some Persian dishes with intriguing exotic smells I was not familiar with. They helped me to develop my culinary skills beyond my  basic knowledge of American college staples like spaghetti, hamburgers, and hot dogs. We also played cards, and I helped them with certain English language problems and customs in America. As I was working on becoming a teacher, this worked out great for me. I became well versed in deconstructing the English language, and explaining local idioms and slang.

I was introduced to a new Iranian student by one of the other Iranians. He had just come to America and had joined our group. Most of the Iranians were into soccer and were of average build, but this guy was a bodybuilder which made him stand out. He could move his pectoral muscles at will and he did so in front of me often. He made me giggle with laughter on many occasions. He made me interested in him, not by his physique, but by his charming antics. His name was Hossein Atrchin-Kashi.

He was working on his master's degree in Business when he came to our school. He graduated in 1982 and turned around and started working on his doctorate degree immediately. We started dating, and even eventually moving in together. Meanwhile, I helped with the typing and grammar in his doctoral thesis, and he helped me keep in shape. We were a team. He made me laugh and I helped him with English. He would translate words from his language (Farsi, or Persian) into funny American expressions for me. For example, popcorn was elephant farts. Eggs were chicken production. Hossein was great at fixing things around the house and keeping our car in tip-top running order. Although he was not fond of animals in general, he fell in love with cats. An expert in patience, he even taught one of our cats how to use the toilet. I thought he was a cat whisperer and was a hoot to

watch play with his cats. They did not have a want in the world. He was going to make a great dad.

My mother and father had been divorced for many years. I drove back and forth from Columbus to Atlanta, GA to visit my dad many times. It was about a hundred miles' drive, but because of my schooling, I only visited when I had the chance. One particular afternoon while Hossein was driving with me from Atlanta back to Columbus on a rainy day something scary happened. As we took a slight curve on the highway going through the mountains we felt our car slide off the road. We drifted into the embankment landing on handful of young pine trees snapping them in half. Frozen in place, Hossein was speechless with his hands still on the wheel seemingly in shock. I was quick to check us for injuries, visually checking the car for damage, and concerned that he was not responding. Believe it or not, we were not seriously injured except for some scrapes and bruises. He eventually snapped out of it and we got down out of the car. We went up to the road, waved down a police officer that happened to be passing through, and he called for a tow truck on his radio. They pulled our car off the trees with the tow line and surprisingly the car was still drivable. It appeared that one of the axles was just lightly bent but we still managed to finish our drive home and get it mended there.

At that point, we had been dating for about three years. After that accident I told him that I wanted to get married. I loved him and if he or I had been injured in that crash we would not be able to help each other in the hospital because we were not direct family members. In fact, he had no family in the states. If nobody was able to help him in an emergency situation, I do not think that it would have turned out well. I did not want to take the chance that I might be parted from him, and he agreed. I am sorry that this decision was not very romantic. It was just very practical, but we were in love.

Hossein and I married on September 7, 1979, in downtown Columbus at the courthouse. A couple of courthouse staff were our witnesses. We didn't have a honeymoon because I was working and we were both in school. We eventually went down to Jekyll Island and other parts of Florida for a delayed honeymoon a month later. During our trip, we were swimming in one of the bay areas of Jekyll Island when I saw Hossein's eyes get very big. He ran as fast as he could to get out of the water. He turned to me and said that something very big and long went between his legs. He was not getting into the water again. I wished that I had a video of his face and body. It was so funny watching him run, hop and jump out of the water. He put his arms up to show how big the fish was that got away between his legs. I laughed all the way home thinking about how he sounded like captain Ahab describing the vicious monster Moby Dick and how it got away.

Of course, on November 4th of the same year, the Iranian hostage crisis happened. Just like everyone else, Hossein and I were bewildered about why this happened. The Iran hostage crisis was a diplomatic standoff between the United States and Iran. Fifty-two American diplomats and citizens were held hostage for 444 days from November 4, 1979, to January 20, 1981. We were extremely worried. Everyone was upset during this situation and we knew that Iranian-Americans were going to get unnecessary backlash. People painted go-home signs on known Iranian cars and houses. Random guys in public would start fights with Iranians. We as humans tend to see a small group of people doing something bad, and we generalize that to the entire group. In this instance, some Americans went overboard and took out their anger on the people of middle eastern descent, regardless of their nationality.

Two months after the Iranian Hostage Crisis began, the National Immigration Service wanted my husband to report to Atlanta with me as his wife. We had applied for a green card for him and we thought that this was why they needed to see us.

Wrong… They were checking up on every Iranian in America. When we reported to Atlanta from Columbus, GA, they separated us into different rooms for interviews. They wanted to know if this was just a marriage for a green card. They asked me if my family knew about our marriage. Did we live together? They even asked me if we were in love with each other. I was glad that I could answer them honestly. Yes, my family knew about us. Yes, we did live together. Yes, I do love him. The process from start to finish lasted for 3–4 hours, between getting there early, waiting in line, and the interviews themselves.

We went back down to Columbus and the Immigration Service did not bother us again but I had a feeling they were keeping an eye on most of the students from Iran at this time. During the next few years since we were married, Iran stayed in the limelight. . After the hostage situation was over, Iraq invaded Iran for  control over the extremely profitable oil fields on their land. It was more complicated than that but it is simple explanation for a complicated situation. Because of the Iranian Hostage Crisis, the American government sided with Iraq and helped with military aid. Of course, many businessmen in America were making money off of this war. We watched the news reports as close as possible. Hossein called home as much as he could but the cost was high, about $7 per minute. Adjusting for inflation to 2023, the cost for the phone calls were about $25 per minute. Meaning that 3-minute phone calls were upwards of $75!

We decided to get our marriage recognized by the Iranian government through the Pakistan Interest section for Iranians living in America at this time. It was located in Washington, D.C. We took a trip up there to show our marriage license and work on getting me an Iranian passport. If I decided to go to Iran, no Americans were allowed in. I had to go in with an Iranian passport. By proving I married Hossein, I was granted Iranian Citizenship. At this point, I was able to have dual citizenship and passports. We even went by the old Iranian embassy where vandals had gotten on the property and painted graffiti all over the building. It had been a beautiful building. It was so sad to see things like this destroyed needlessly.

Hossein began to work on his doctorate's degree just right after he obtained his master's degree from Columbus College. He had just finished up the degree before he had a call from his brother in Iran that his mother had a stroke in 1983. At the time, I was also about four months pregnant. He was unsure about if his mother would live or die, so he needed to go to see her. His father died when he was very young but he had one older brother and sister who were taking care of her. He was the baby of the family and his mother was very dear to him. I understood how much he loved her, and why seeing her was very important. We talked about going there together to stay for a while but he put that idea on hold until he got there and checked out how safe it was. He was not sure how the war was affecting the living conditions.

He got to Iran in November of '83 and his mother was still alive. We were happy. She was now partially paralyzed on one side of her body but she was alert and could move around a little. His brother and sister appreciated that he had come home to help. His brother was a civil engineer and worked a lot. His sister was a principal at an elementary school. They had very busy careers and it was hard to take care of his mother.

At this point, the war was very quiet. Nothing was happening in Tehran. It was all on the western border with Iraq. That was where the action was occurring. Hossein talked to me again about coming. He explained that he had cousins that were doctors in Tehran. I could  come and deliver the baby there. He thought that the war would end soon. I discussed it with my family about my going. All of my friends and acquaintances had a preconceived notion of Iran. They did not trust the people. All of the news on TV was not kind to that part of the world. My dad asked why I wanted to go. I explained to him that he had traveled all over the world for his military job. He had been in Korea's cold war, two years in Vietnam, and in Germany in the aftermath of WW ll. My brother came home in a casket from Vietnam. He was reluctant for me to go. I told him it was my time to see the world. He was suspicious of the government there but told me to go for t. He would worry, but he understood.

We started to plan. Hossein got it arranged to have all of his and my household stuff shipped to Iran. It was about five large boxes, each roughly the size of a standard washing machine. I had to take them to the Atlanta International shipping area at the airport. It was all paid on the other end by Hossein. The guys that check my stuff in, thought it was very strange. I guessed that they thought that I was sending something illegal to Iran. I laughed and showed them my kitchen stuff and clothes. I told them that I was lucky that my husband had gotten permission to pay for the shipping from over there. The cost was a lot less paid in Iranian Rials compared to American dollars.

Hossein sent me a ticket to come. My flight was on February 5th, 1984. I was about 5 ½ months pregnant at this point. I was showing but was able to fly and travel. Hossein told me to wear a long coat, pants, and a scarf to cover my hair. I traveled on an American plane to Germany and then got on an Iranian plane in Frankfurt. That is when I put my scarf and coat on. The journey was long but I was so excited to be finally exploring a different part of the world.

It was now the law of Iran that all women had to cover their bodies and hair. In the '70s in Iran, it had been very open and free for a woman. If they wanted to wear European clothes out, they could. They even wore mini-skirts. But with a new religious government, all things for women were changed. A lot of people did not like western customs. They believed that Iranian women had gone too far and were not modest in their clothes and partying ways. It was like having a catholic family who was 100 years back in time. They wanted women to be conservative in their ways. I was a little old-fashion anyway so it did not bother me too much. I was more into nerdy things like geology and archaeology. I loved learning about the history and cultures of places around the world. Drinking liquor and going out dancing would not be missed as far as I was concerned.

One thing that stood out about me was my blue eyes. My husband warned me not to look at men directly. I could avert my eyes from looking at men directly when talking to them. I would get more respect from men if I was modest in my actions. Everyone would be interested in looking at the color of my eyes so I would get unneeded attention. I was traveling alone so I had to be careful. He tried to give me the best advice on coming into the country and how to react to the people in charge now. They were at war with Iraq and no Americans were allowed. I had to put my American passport somewhere in my bags so no one would take it from me.

English became the second dominant language after French in Iran around the 1950s. The French had their hands in Iranian affairs since the 1700s. If you ever go there, even though the signs are in English, the pronunciation was French. The word 'Iran' is a good example. In English, we say I – ran. The correct pronunciation is E – ron.

3

A Little Background
Info on Hossein

Before I continue on my flight going into Iran, let me give you a little background information on my husband. Hossein went into detail about his family to help me to learn and understand more about them. His family came from the town of Kashan, and they had been there for many generations. He showed me the only picture of his father he had. His father died when Hossein was a very little boy and could remember very little about him. His father died from maybe pneumonia but back then in the early 1950s, nobody knew for sure. The small town of Kashan did not have advanced medication like we had in America at that time. Antibiotics could have made the difference and he could

have lived a longer life, but they were not widely available during that time period. All Hossein could recall is that his father had a garden in the small village of Ghomsar where 

he grew Mohammadi tea roses for making rose water. He would then sell the water in the Kashan bazaar.

He did not mention any other family from his dad's side of the family. His mother's family tree was a sprawling spider web. They were pretty well-known as one of the older families that had been in Kashan for a long time. Their family name was Mofidi and many of them were very religious in their own right. The grandfather was a religious leader, arbitrated countless civil disputes, and was a figurehead of the community. He had four sons and a couple of daughters, one of them being Hossein's mother. Most of the brothers did not follow in their  father's footsteps and instead became business men. Hossein's mother was very much a traditional housewife. Before she knew who she would wed, she had started her dowry, which involved creates many different kinds of household goods. She creates cut-out patterns on pillowcases and table covers and sews together blankets. Many women were prized as good brides if they were able to create carpets. Hossein's mother was from a well-known family so she was already a prize without having to working on carpets. Carpet making was painstaking work and tended to shorten women's lifespans.

In Hossein's direct family, his mother had three sons and one daughter. Her second son had died in a tragic accident and she honored him, by gifting his name and birthday to her third son. That was Hossein. Hossein was 26 legally older by about three years than he actually was, because his dead brother's birth certificate became his. He could only guess when he was born. Back then, babies were typically born at home, so there were no official hospital documents. We figured that he was about seven years older than me.

The eldest son, Mohammad, had just gotten a well-paying job in Tehran as civil engineer which sparked Hossein's family to move away their ancestral home to join him. They liquidated their holdings in Kashan, in order to fund their move to Tehran. He had his degree in civil engineering, was proficient in his work, was respected highly, and had a magnetic personality. He had purchased a two story apartment building, that functioned as two full separate apartments. One was for himself and his wife, and the other for mother and siblings. The sister, Shirin got a job at a school as a principal, while Hossein worked on his business undergraduate in Tehran.

Hossein's uncle practiced an old Iranian type of athletics and martial arts now known as Varzesh-e Bastani. He loved to go to the House of Strength, the Zurkhaneh, to practice a freestyle type of wrestling called Koshti Pahlevani. What I found interesting were the Indian clubs (meels in Persian) he used. They were shaped like huge bowling pins weighing from a few pounds up to a hundred. They were used in a type of choreography of routines in which an announcer would play a beat on a drum and chant certain phases from the Shahnameh epic, Koran, or other ancient texts. The clubs were swung in unison by the group of athletes in a circle. This sport was seen as a way to promote inner strength through outer strength. He told me that anyone who learned to wrestle in this sport was someone who embodied kindness and humility while defending society from evil. It gave him focus and purpose in life. This philosophy endured with him all the years I knew him.

In the early '70s, just like many of his fellow students, Hossein wanted something to change in Iran. The current Shah (king) was not very popular with the average citizen. According to the word on the street, the American CIA had organized a coup. They installed Mohammad Reza Pahlavi as Shah in order to secure American business interests in Iranian oil fields. You could get away with a lot of illegal things if you were a favorite of the Shah. Back in that time, Americans were very popular and the Iranian people felt betrayed by foreign interference in their government, and their lives.

There was large-scale unrest in Iran during 1970s. The Shah had a secret police force called the SAVAK. They did a lot of unpopular and devious things to keep the population under control. People would all of a sudden disappear or be thrown into jail for a bogus charge. Many of Hossein's fellow college students started to protest and march in the streets against the Shah as they demanded change. Hossein eventually decided to join them in protest. In one of those marches, the soldiers broke up the protest and arrested some of the students, including Hossein. They hosed them down with a powerful water hose, and were all beaten up egregiously. Once they were in jail and recovering, Hossein stood out like a sore thumb. He looked like a young Arnold Schwarzenegger amidst the crowd of average student frames. A military captain pulled Hossein out of his cell in

order to have a conversation about life and the direction he was heading. Regardless of his true intentions, the captain had made such a good impression on him, so much so that when he was released from jail, Hossein never protested again. He decided that it was more important to focus on his future and his family's future rather than get caught up in political unrest. Once he grown and established himself, maybe he could help influence his country towards a better future. From these experiences, he taught me the expression "Don't show your whole hand to everyone." Meaning always lie a little to those you don't trust. Tell half-truths until you get to know someone. If everybody knows your next move, it's easy to get played.

He finished his undergraduate degree in business and then went into the Iranian military service for two years which was required by all students after graduation. He was stationed in southern Iran during his tour of duty. He

enjoyed the discipline of the military and was proud of his marching ability. He luckily never saw any action during his duty, but boy did they

love marching! They even had a picture of his squad marching in front of a picture of the Shah since he couldn't be there. He focused on getting his body in shape instead of politics. It was a quiet time for him in his two-year service in the military.

Iran had American oil companies working almost everywhere, so English-speaking foreigners were very commonplace in the population. Interacting with many of these people got Hossein really interested in studying abroad. He started to learn English with the plans of going to America for his master's degree in business after his military service was over. He got in to America on a student visa and started college in Atlanta. He eventually got accepted into Columbus College in Columbus, Georgia where I met him. While he was away, a revolution began against the puppet government and the reigning Shah. There was an Iranian religious leader called Ayatollah Ruhollah Khomeini who had been exiled many years ago, and was currently living in France. Khomeini was an Ayatollah, a high ranking clergy member, and had a surprisingly profound impact on the hearts of many Iranians. Khomeini encouraged the people to join hands in solidarity against the corrupt Shah, as he considered the Shah to be evil and decadent in the ways he lived. According to Khomeini, the Shah was not a good king and could not lead his people righteously. Mohammad Reza Pahlavi, the acting Shah, was the central decision maker and almost nothing in government could be done without his approval. He had secretly been diagnosed with cancer almost 4 years ago and his mind was being affected by the treatment, leaving his decisions to be rash and unstable. A temperamental king who effectively had full control of the government, made it impossible to try to quell any uprising. Much to Hossein's chagrin, Ayatollah Khomeini returned to Iran on February 1, 1979, only 1 month after the Shah abandoned Iran to seek treatment.

During the days after the Shah left the country, a lot of people wanted revenge on the corrupt people that were in power during the Shah. Anyone who was in a high office or upper ranks of the military were going to have a lot of problems. Hossein's brother, Mohammad, had married a lady whose father was a high-ranking officer. Mohammad and his wife had two small children when the overthrow happened, and everyone on his wife's side of the family became scared. They were afraid for their lives and planned to leave the country and go to France. In Iran, when a woman leaves the country, they have to have permission from their husband, which also applied to the kids. Somehow the parents were able to take Mohammad's wife and kids out of the country without Mohammad permission. He did not know where they were for weeks. He was distraught as he searched all the hospitals, police departments, and anywhere else they could have gone. He thought that they had been taken by the police, kidnapped, or dead somewhere. Finally, his wife called him from France explaining that her family was afraid for their lives and that they had to leave. She pleaded him to come to France to join them, but he couldn't, as he had too many responsibilities for his own mother and family in Iran. He was extremely sad and angry that she had kept it a secret. He would eventually go to visit her and the kids in the near future, but the airports were shut down, and it was generally too dangerous to leave. He visited his wife and kids many times over the years, but he eventually decided to divorce. He knew that her family would take care of them, and by divorcing her, he freed her of her duties to him so she could have a normal life in France. A few years later Mohammad married a lady named Ava and started a new family, although he did keep in contact with his kids in France.

It was a stressful time for a lot of people, especially in Iran. Because of the government destabilization, Iranians didn't know if their job was safe or if they could even put food on the table. Because his family was on the religious side of this turmoil, Hossein felt relatively confident that they would be safe. Back in America, Hossein focused on finishing his Master's degree at Columbus College and did an online course for his Ph.D. in business. He avoided talking about what was happening in Iran for fear being associated with either side and decided to just stay out of it. And of course, I helped him in typing and checking the grammar in his thesis. I did not finish my degree until many years later.

Major locations mentioned in the story.

4

First Day in Iran
February 5, 1984

Returning back to my part of the story, I had to tie up loose ends here in the states before I left for Iran. I was not sure when we would return. I gave my car to my niece in Atlanta to take care of and started the first leg of the expedition which lasted about nine hours. I flew from the Atlanta International Airport into Frankfurt Germany on American Airlines and then switched to Iran-Air for the flight into Tehran. I had to put on my scarf before I got on the second plane. Luckily, it was February so I was already wearing my pants and coat which covered my legs and arms as you do in Iran for modest dress. The people on board looked a little surprised at me traveling alone. One or two of the Iranians on the plane were very friendly and talked to me in English. It was another long flight of about eight hours. The food on Iran-Air was different than your typical airline fair. The taste of stew over rice had a great flavor that I was not accustomed to and was a nice change of pace. I was tired and excited at the same time, so much so that I could not sleep. I kept my eyes glued to the window to see the lights and terrain of the places we were flying over. I had never flown on a plane before and it was thrilling to experience two of them back to back. Although I was a little nervous about the takeoff and landings, I was flying almost half the way around the world. That in itself was remarkable. I had seen most of the United States by car, but now I was seeing half of the world by plane.

The plane finally landed and all of the passengers debarked off the plane in the late evening. We had to get a shuttle bus to take us to the terminal. All of the people rushed to get carts and get their luggage off of the carousel and get through checkout. I was almost six months pregnant and no one offered to help me get a cart or get my luggage off the carousel. All of the carts were snatched within a few minutes, and I just waited patiently. Back in this time, suitcases with wheels were rare, and I had none so it was difficult to carry, especially while pregnant. I looked around and saw many pictures of the religious leader, Khomeini on the walls. There were anti-American sayings on the walls, too. It was a very cold and sad-looking terminal.

Finally, one family took pity on me. The father asked me in English if he could help me get a cart for my luggage. I was almost in tears. "Yes, please," I thanked him so much. I slowly pushed my cart to customs with my two full suitcases. I think that I was the last passenger off of the plane still trying to checkout of the terminal. I did not know this at the time, but Hossein was able to get a view of me from the second-floor balcony while I was waiting for help. He was wondering if I had made my flight since it took me so long to go through customs, so he went up to look for me.

The customs checkout was very interesting. I spoke no Farsi at this point and the agent checking me out did not speak any English. He gestured for me open my luggage. In my luggage I mostly had clothes for my baby and I, as well as toys. He was very bemused by these strange foreign toys, as he picked them up and played with them. I pointed to my stomach to explain they were for my baby. He seemed to smile and after a few more checks of my things and fiddling with the toys, he let me pass through the gate.

Hossein was waiting around the corner from customs, behind some stanchions. He had been so anxious about not being able to help me. He looked around, hugged me and gave me a very short kiss. We had not seen each other for over four months. He explained to me that one should not show affection out in public to each other. We would have to wait until we had gotten into the car before we could have a loving embrace. My brother-in-law Mohammad and my sister-in-law Shirin had also come along to greet me. She had surprised me with some flowers and gave me a kiss on each one of my cheeks. People of the same sex could peck each other on the cheeks as a traditional greeting and was not considered taboo. Shaking hands was not a standard greeting in Iran, and if you did, they knew you were a foreigner. They were so welcoming to me after that long journey, I felt like I had come home. I did not feel like a stranger.

Mohammad had an old American car. It was a white Chevrolet Rambler from about 1967. The car was nice and roomy with plenty of room to get my two bulging suitcases into the trunk and we then were off. I had come very late in the night and did not get out of the terminal until early morning. I wanted so much to see the sites along the way but I could not. The only thing that I saw was the Freedom monument (Azadi tower). It was lit up like the Eiffel Tower in Paris, and decorated the dark morning sky. I wanted so badly to see and visit it during the daytime.

It was almost dawn when we got to their dwelling which looked more like an apartment. Mohammad dropped us off at the door while he parked the car at the back entrance. Hossein walked me inside and I took off my shoes in the entranceway. I was already used to not wearing shoes inside the house as we practiced that tradition in Columbus in our old home. The Iranians and Japanese have many customs in common. Being very clean is next to Godliness. So you will see a various selection of shoes from the family members right before you go into the main room, as trekking in dirt makes it impossible to pray. Animals like dogs were considered unclean. You do not find too many dogs inside an Iranian home.

I met my mother-in-law and my brother-in-law's wife, Ava with her little two-year-old girl daughter. By this time, I had very little sleep. Hossein led me to a bed in one of the bedrooms in the back. The mattress was hard as a rock but

I didn't care. I was exhausted and immediately fell asleep in Hossein's arms. It felt so great that everything else melted away.

When I finally woke up, it was in the afternoon. I looked out the window and peered out at the buildings around me. Everything was a monotone grey or cream wash of color. Ladies wearing black and flowery coverings called chadors were walking on the sidewalks with small kids. A tiny little store was at the corner near our building. Some men were there buying things from the store but what they were purchasing was a big mystery to me. There was snow covering the ground in patches, and the sidewalk was a little icy.

I got up and went into the living room. My mother-in-law had a bedroll on the floor. It was more like a pallet of cotton covered with fabric with a round long pillow against the wall, comparable to a Japanese futon. There were bolster pillows to put your back against to be comfortable. There were some chairs in the room but almost everyone shared the floor with their mother, since she couldn't standup from a stroke she had in the past. She spoke no English but she was very kind to me. She gave me kisses and hugs and welcomed me to the family. My sister-in-law Shirin made us some food, then I unpacked and settled in.

Let me explain our building. Mohammad and Shirin owned it. It was a two story apartment complex that had a separate residence upstairs and downstairs. I lived with Hossein, his mother, and his sister on the first floor.

Mohammad and Ava with their daughter were on the second floor. We had a flight of stairs enclosed on the inside of the building but outside of each apartment. When we went inside the entrance, there was a separate shoe rack in front of each apartment, one on the first floor and one of the second. We would leave our shoes in whichever shoe rack was outside of the apartment we were entering and then go in barefoot. There was also a flight of stairs going to the top of the building which had a flat roof that we could walk on.

There was a small backyard that could only fit one car and a raised garden bed on the other side. There was a ten feet wall that surrounded the backyard so we could be comfortable in the backyard with very few people able to see us. We had a back porch that we could go out on to sit. We had adjacent apartments right next to us like a suite of high-rise condominiums. We lived on a side street between major boulevards and about a mile from a major thoroughfare so that we could get taxis and buses. We were about five miles from the Freedom Tower and about fifteen miles from the Tehran airport.

Our apartment had a bathroom, a shower room, two small bedrooms, a dining room, a living room, and makeshift kitchen with a sink and one set of cabinets in it. These apartments were not equipped with traditional appliances like a stove like we do in America. We had a table with eight chairs and a large crystal chandelier over the table. We never used the table to eat at, it was simply

decorative. The table and chair were foreign furniture and they were not accustomed to using them. They preferred the floor, so we put a large plastic tablecloth on the floor to be our table. Now remember, that they wore no shoes in the house and vacuumed daily, so the floors were always in pristine condition.

We had large beautiful Persian carpets on all of the floors. Only the toilet and shower room had tiles. The windows were high up on the wall so no one could look inside the house. Curtains were on all of the windows, too. There were no built-in closets but they used armoires to store their clothes and other personal items.

They did not have a lot of clothes as we do in America. They were very limited in their storage space, so they had to be careful with the amount of items they acquired. We had the only proper bed in the downstairs apartment. Shirin slept on a cotton pallet near her mother. We had fancy pillows sewn together with Persian carpet about the size of a 35-inch flat screen TV located in various rooms for visitors to sit and lean against, several of which resided in the living room.

Within the next couple of days, Shirin went to buy some material for a chador (veil) for me. She needed about five meters and of course, it would be a type of black polyester material. She also purchased some white flowery cotton material for a second chador to use around the house. The black one was more formal and I would wear it outside anywhere I went. She taught

me how to measure, cut, and assemble them. We tested the length of the material against my height. I was only 5'3" but a little taller than Shirin. The final product, needed to be a half circle with a radius equal to my height, however the material we had purchased was only about 4'6" wide. Which required us to cut a second piece to stitch to the other half, but keep the curve of the half circle in the process. It was a fun way to bond with my sister-in-law.

Shirin's mother had an old hand-cranked, non-foot pedal, sewing machine that Shirin taught me how to use. I was well trained in using electric sewing machines, so it was not difficult to adjust to this antiquated version. This older machine lacked several safety features found in more current models. There was a larger distance between the needle and base plate that could allow for thicker materials, however this was non-adjustable, and without a safeguard it was easy for your finger to slip between the fabric and needle. In America, a lot of products come with safety measures and warning to avoid lawsuits, and this loosely referred to as "Idiot proofing". I was an idiot that was operating a non-idiot proof device, and my thumb was sacrificed to the needle. It was terrible to not be able to move your hand as its impaled by a sewing machine you are now one with. I called for my sister-in-law to help get Vlad the Impaler off me. The pain hadn't hit me yet and I couldn't believe my eyes, as she cranked the machine that raised the needle out of my thumb. After getting patched up, and the blood sacrifice was made, I got back on the horse and kept sewing. I finished my work on the first chador and then completed the second one without issue.

My thoughts went back to that scene in the movie *Lawrence of Arabia*, again where Peter O'Toole is dancing in the desert with his new clothes on. He held his light loose garments up to the sun and sang. I felt the same way with my chador. I wore several things whenever I went out, undergarments, typical American street clothes which consisted of a long-sleeved shirt and long pants, a scarf, a chador, and sandals. I modeled in the mirror, how I would hold myself while wearing the Chador. It was not fashionable for the women to pin their chador in place, so you had to hold it in place, meaning you only one hand free at any given moment. I wore the scarf under the chador to hide my hair in the event my veil slipped. Shirin showed me how to wrap the ends of the cotton chador around my neck, exposing my arms, so I could use both my hands to sweep outside. Generally, a Chador is meant to cover almost every part of a women's body barring the hands and face, however exceptions we made when a woman needed to work around the house.

During the summer it was very hot with all of this garb on. Not being used to the extreme 100+ degree weather, I was constantly taking showers to cool myself down whenever I got back home fearing heat exhaustion. The average Iranian might get away without a taking a shower by splashing their face with water and/or drinking hot tea which they claimed helped cool themselves down.

Hossein pointed out to me that when we were sitting down on the floor, that in order to be courteous I must keep the soles of my feet away from anyone else. It was an insult to put your feet in front of someone, instead you should kneel, cross your legs, or side sit. That took me a good while to practice and remember. I was not very comfortable being pregnant and sitting on the floor all the time. I was becoming more agile except for my knees. My family had a history of bad and sore knees and I was going the same route.

They had a small TV with an antenna, but of the programs available, nothing interested me. It was mostly news about the war and Mullahs (a lower ranking male religious leader) teaching how to be a proper Shi'ite Muslim (which was the accepted religious practice in Iran). In the news, a common theme they showed was people demonstrating against the Western foreign powers and what was occurring Iran-Iraq war. They honored the martyred soldiers from the war and celebrated their bravery. The TV only received programming from 2pm to 8pm, otherwise it was just static. The Mullahs would sometimes perform or chant songs, but only about religion or the war. At this point, I rarely saw any women except for a newscaster or two. Later on, the only thing that we watched on a regular basis was Madrese Mooshha (Mice School). It was a bunch of puppet mice telling jokes about school, and Hossein would translate for me. It was the only cute thing on TV that was age-appropriate for kids to watch. They eventually went on to make a movie with the mice characters.

I was adjusting well, however the only major problem I had was dreaming at night that I was out on the public street without my veil. The feeling was equivocal to having the dream of going to school naked. In the dream I felt very nervous about my missing head covering and I was afraid that I would be arrested. That dream looming large in my mind, made me extremely paranoid of the veil covering my hair. Being from an old traditional family, my sister-in-law demonstrated how to hide my blonde hair. This helped me ensure that my veil was always fully covering my hair instead of partially like other Iranian women that didn't mind. This lead to most people thinking that I was very modest and followed the religion carefully. Ava, my other sister-in-law did not wear a chador. She had traveled outside of Iran and liked the more modern long jacket, pants, and large rectangular scarf to cover her head.

I was a little jealous of her and asked Hossein about this difference. Why should I wear the chador instead of what Ava was wearing? His answer was short and simple. Being a blonde-haired, blue-eyed American, I stuck out like a sore thumb. It would be a lot easier to blend in, and people would be more respectful towards me. Well, he did make some sense. In America I had been modest in the style of clothing I wore there, so I should do the same in Iran. I wore shorts all the time in America, but in Iran I could only do so in the privacy of my own bedroom. I considered my home to be like my little America, a place where I could truly be free and relaxed, while on the streets I present my Iranian facade.

5

Staying Fit with 1940's Appliances

I need a chapter dedicated to the everyday items that we have in our lives in Iran. That way we can get rid of the exposition in one fell swoop. Otherwise, I will be going back and forth to explain these real life issues as they relate to my story. I know that not all Americans have some of the things that I am about to talk about, but most do. The appliances I had access to really kept me in shape, primarily because nothing was easy. You cannot really appreciate having these items in your everyday life until you have been deprived of them.

Again, I was six months pregnant when I first came to Iran. I had only traveled outside the country to Ciudad Juarez, Mexico for grocery shopping while we lived in El Paso, Texas. I had not experienced bathrooms that were fundamentally different than those found in the United States. My husband had tried to describe what they looked like to me, but with no success. Now, it is my turn to describe them to you.

Let's start with the toilet. My husband had told me that it was a hole in the floor of a bathroom. You did not use toilet paper to wipe yourself. You used water. I just said, "ew." Hossein took me into the toilet room which I could best describe as a half bath. There was a normal sink and a toilet bowl recessed into the floor with rugged footholds on the sides of the rim instead of smooth porcelain. The floor and sides of the wall were tiled like a shower stall. There was also a short water hose with on/off valves. The tank of the toilet was raised and installed on the wall connected by a pipe to the bowl in the floor. There was also a chain instead of a handle on the tank, that dangled within reach when you stood up. From what my husband had told me, this was an upscale toilet. I later confirmed that fact to my horror.

He explained how to use it in detail. I turned around to face the door, had my feet straddling the rugged sides of the toilet, and then squatted. Just pause and think about that for a moment. I was six months pregnant and never needed to squat in this manner before. Between lack of squatting muscles and the small human growing in my belly, I needed all the help I could get in order to relieve myself. I was able to put one hand on the sink and the other hand on the wall to help balance myself. I straddled and squatted as gracefully as my big belly would allow me. I did my business and then reached for the water hose with my right hand still on the sink. I turned it on and sprayed my bottom. It was cold water, and the pressure was quite high. I then had to take my right hand and wipe myself clean, while I balanced on my feet, and continued to operate the hose with my left hand. This is probably the best time to let everyone know that I am a left handed person, and in the Muslim culture, you eat with your right hand and you wipe yourself with the left hand for sanitary reasons. My husband explained that I would shake myself dry, and that there was warm water and I just had to learn to adjust it. I did get used to it but I added a towel to my routine to dry myself. There was no toilet paper! The final step was to flush the toilet via the chain. There was no fan or air freshener to clear any smells away so I put some cologne in the room to spray when needed.

When traveling, most of the toilets were not as nice as the one at home. Some of the bathrooms were just holes in the ground without any running water. You had to go find a water source, fill it with a plastic watering can that sat in the bathroom, and then take it in with you to do your business. The bathroom smells were horrific. You never had had to ask where the toilet was, you just knew. You could easily smell the direction of the public toilet from far away and you tried to hold your breath the whole time you were in there.

The other part of the traditional bathroom is the shower/bathing area. In the first place we lived, it was in a separate room from the toilet. It had a glass and metal door that was raised off the floor so water couldn't escape. The room was tiled like a large shower stall and there was a drain in the middle of the floor to take all of the water away. There were no shower heads but only a hose with the option for hot and cold water. My in-laws had a very small kiddie pool on the floor in the shower to sit next to and pour cups of water over their heads to clean themselves. You would go in there once or twice a week to have a bath/shower.

There was a problem in Tehran with these washrooms. In the middle of the night, hundreds of large roaches would come out of the drain, and presumably feast on whatever we had left behind. We had to keep the bathroom door shut at all times. I know in Georgia we had a cockroach problem but this was magnitudes worse. Peering into the bathroom through the glass window of the door evoked a horrific sight, as the walls and floor moved in a sickening organic fashion. I had to laugh at how many roommates I had gained, and none paid rent! On one occasion, one of the horde escaped his confinement and bit my arm in the middle of the night. That was a first for me.

We also never had a washing machine and god forbid a dryer! Washing machines did exist there, but only to the wealthiest of families. So that small kiddie pool in the shower room was where I washed my clothes. Boy I was glad that I was still young and healthy because of how much work it took to wash clothes by hand, especially when handwashing cloth diapers. I didn't have to use that much soap, as our clothes were not very dirty, just sweaty. For that aspect I am grateful, as getting soap out of clothes manually is difficult work. When we hung up clothes to dry on the clotheslines in the backyard, they would dry like I had put starch on them. In Tehran, there was black soot in the air, and in Kashan, we would have sand storms. So as soon as the clothes were dry you needed to get them back inside.

The next appliance I want to talk about is dishwashers. Of course, I did not have one, I was one. These machines were almost unheard of in Iran. We definitely did not have enough luxury money to buy these things, although I did see them in the homes of more affluent families.

The kitchen setup in Iran can vary from home to home. The first kitchen I was introduced to was very basic. It was a small 12-foot square room. They had installed a metal kitchen sink unit, consisting of only two upper cabinets and two lower cabinets with a sink in the middle. They had refrigerator about 5 feet in height, with a very small freezer on top. Both of these items were reminiscent of the 1950s American era. Instead of a standard stove that allows for baking, we only had a double burner stove similar to one you might have while camping. It was hooked up to a large propane tank, which we had to refill at least twice a month. Basically, you were using a gas grill that sat on tiny table barely 11 inches off the ground. You did not stand to do your cooking, you sat on the floor. You used cutting boards to work on the floor and there were no table or chairs in the kitchen. When visiting my mother-in-law's house over the course of the 4 years I lived in Iran, we only once used her fancy table and chairs once. Iranians in general preferred to put a plastic tablecloth down on the carpeted floor and serve there. The repeated up and down nature of daily Iranian life is what I blame my bad knees on today.

6

Having My Baby

After talking about bathrooms and toilets, I have to remind you that I was very pregnant. Making it difficult in many facets of life here in Iran. With that being said, I survived this drastic change in lifestyle amidst my pregnancy and came out stronger and more determined to succeed in life. I had about 3 months left before I was scheduled to deliver. My sister-in-law got me an appointment with an Iranian doctor who only spoke Farsi and German. I could not speak German and my Farsi was very limited so I had to have my husband translate everything when we met the doctor.

Getting to the doctor's office was a challenge. There are two things of abundance in Iran, roundabouts and taxis. We had to walk more than a mile to a nearby roundabout, where anyone could pick up almost any kind of transportation. Our first taxi took us halfway there, dropping us off at a second roundabout, requiring us to flag down a second taxi to take us the rest of the We were dropped off within a block of the doctor's office and walked the rest of the way. The rooms were very bare. It was very grey and sobering in color. It did not evoke a sense of cheer or warmth that modern doctors' offices we have in America. There was some basic furniture and a receptionist to check us in. I remained fully veiled head to toe, while the doctor listened to my baby's heartbeat through the thin cloth. He asked a little about my family's medical history and if I was up-to-date on my shots. Everything was fine from what he could see. I was to see him again in about six weeks. We returned home and began to convert our living space to accommodate a newborn.

Prejudice can go both ways, especially amid escalating tensions. In Tehran, I experienced prejudice, but most of the time it was not born of pure hatred. It was that Iranians had a preconception that all American women were akin to valley girls, women who came from California and lived a luxurious life. We had problems in America when the hostage crisis occurred. People were afraid to have Iranians around them. They wanted all Iranians to be deported because of what had happened at the American Embassy and the hostages that were held for a year. Many Americans hated all Iranians, prejudice born from hatred.

I remember when Hossein would apply for jobs in Tehran, unable to get any work. They would say, "Oh, you're married to an American. She'll want to go home soon, she won't last." I always thought that they never gave their own culture enough credit. There are many things that were special about Iran. The traditions, culture, and history of these areas fascinated me. I loved history. I wanted to learn and research everything. Yes, they were prejudiced against foreigners. They did not want to hire someone that would not last long. They did not know me very well and some Americans can be from hardy stock. I did not go to nightclubs or miss drinking alcoholic beverages. I knew how to sew, knit and create things. I knew hard work and how to stretch my money to the end of the month.

Hossein went on many interviews in Tehran with no luck. He finally decided to see if he could get a job in the old city of Kashan where his family was originally from. It is about 150 miles and a long three-hour drive. He went on a bus to get there. He left Tehran about three weeks before my due date. He was going to stay with his cousin and his aunt while he searched. I told him not to be gone more than a week just in case the baby came early. Right before he left, he said, "I will be back in plenty of time," – famous last words!

During the week he was gone, I kept busy. I would babysit my niece. I got my sewing machine out and sewed on some things for the crib. We had brought a small crib just a few days before he went on his trip. I had brought a mobile from America to put on the top of the crib. I had brought some Winnie-the-Poo Bear things to decorate with. I was definitely nesting and getting ready for the baby.

The week was finally about up. Hossein had promised me that he would be back in the evening. I had been watching and waiting near the door. I was excited to see him again. The phone rang and Monir answered. I was not sure what the conversation was about until she motioned me to the phone. It was Hossein. He thought that he had a job but he had to go to a second interview the very next morning. He would come home tomorrow evening. My heart dropped. I was so looking forward to seeing him this evening but I understood. He needed a job to support us. I told him that I loved him and would be waiting for him.

I ate dinner quietly. I let Shirin talk to her mother in Farsi with no interruptions. She still had not learned much English but I had been working on my Farsi. I made her say the words of things in the house in Farsi and I would write the pronunciation. Tonight, I did not want to do anything. I started to feel tired and told everyone that I was going to bed early.

I was feeling unsettled. I thought that I was depressed. It was still two weeks before my due date but I felt that something was not right. This was my first baby and I had no experience in understanding my body. My back was hurting a little. I did not know that contractions could have an effect on my back. I waited about two hours and then I realized that I was in labor. My husband was not here. I felt very alone.

I woke up Shirin and pointed to my stomach. She was surprised and then woke up Mohammad and Ava in the upstairs apartment. Ava looked at me and also thought that I was in labor by the symptoms I was showing. Mohammad got dressed and called the doctor and the hospital. He got the car out of the backyard. Shirin came with me and Ava stayed home with her daughter. It was about 11 o'clock at night. I knew that there was no way that Hossein could get to the hospital on time if I was about to deliver.

We were going to the Pasteur Hospital in the middle of Tehran. It was about a thirty-minute drive and we had no traffic that time of the evening. By the time we got there, I was bent over in pain. Shirin helped me in while Mohammed checked us in. Once we were checked, the nurses took me into a labor room with three other ladies who were also getting to the point of having their babies. I was gowned up and given a rectal enema to clear any stool. I lived in the bathroom for a while. Boy, did that clean me out.

Shirin was not allowed inside with me, so I had nobody to comfort me. The nurses and doctor were the only company I had, and nobody spoke English. They all wore white short head coverings with their faces unveiled, and long white jackets and pants. They were very nice to me. They spoke only a few words of English. In Farsi I said hello to the other ladies in labor and wished them all the best of luck. I noticed throughout of the course of the night that I was the quietest one in the room and the other women were screaming and shouting in pain. I suffered mostly in silence.

My doctor finally came at about 4 a.m. in the morning. My contractions were getting to be about four minutes apart. The nurse who was helping me turned to the doctor and said how white I was down in the pelvic region. He explained to her that this was normal for more fair-skinned foreigners. I must have been the first foreigner she had dealt with. All of this conversion was in Farsi. I was beginning to understand a few words but not a whole conversation.

As my contractions got shorter, I could tell as well as the staff, that I was beginning to crown. They rowed my bed into a small private room and got me ready. The doctor was in position and said something to me. I was puzzled. I did not understand because of the pain I was having through my contractions. I was not given any kind of pain medication. One of the nurses tried to translate for me. He says, "Push," she said to the best of her ability. I could only laugh through my pain and began to push.

At about 5:45 am in the morning, my dear little girl was born. Hossein and I had already discussed naming her Angela if she was a girl and Ali Alexander if a boy. So, Angela, it was. The only problem was she was delivered two weeks early. She weighed only four pounds. She was otherwise very healthy. She had a little jaundice and they put her into a baby monitoring station. I got to kiss her right above her right eyebrow before they took her. I will always call that part of her forehead her sweet spot. She was so delicate and skinny. I was very concerned and wished that I could hold her. I knew that it was for the best that she went to the station.

I was in a recovery room when Shirin was able to join me. I explained as best as I could about Angela, but I think the nurse had already explained things to her. I knew that Hossein did not know that he was a father yet. I asked Shirin to go home and call Hossein. I asked her to make sure he got the first bus back in the morning. If she called him and let him know now, he could take a 3-hour bus, and easily be back in Tehran by noon. She was willing to stay with me but I wanted to get Hossein here as soon as possible. I had no sleep from the night before so I thought that I would could crash at any minute. So, she did as I asked, and left.

I was put into a room with about five other ladies who had had their babies, too. I was the closest to the back wall. I could see all of the babies with their mothers. Angela was too small and needed to be watched. I was truly alone and depressed. I tried to sleep but I was too stressed out by the events that I had gone through. By mid-day, I was in tears. I tried to hide how upset I was, but one of the nurses noticed my red eyes. She tried to comfort me but I could not explain why I was upset.

I saw no one until about 7 p.m. when Hossein finally arrived. As I broke down in tears while he held me, I asked him why it took him so long. He claimed that Shirin did not call him until midday, and that meant he was unable to get a ticket until later in the afternoon due to buses being full. He was livid because no one told him sooner. I snapped back at him, that he promised to be here, but was instead was delayed in Kashan. It was not entirely his fault, but I would rather him be mad at himself than to take it out on his family.

I spilled my guts and dark thoughts to him about how I was so alone. No family, all alone in a foreign country, and no one able to speak English to me was the worst feeling, as if I had fallen into a deep void. I was dispirited and forlorn over Angela's fate all day. I was spiraling, my mind racing, creating every terrible scenario that was possible. Was she still alive, was she breathing on her own, did she miss me, was she being taken care of, or was she just some sideshow attraction? No one could tell me, nobody could listen, and it felt like nobody cared. After I finished emotionally dumping all of this on Hossein, he immediately went to see his daughter. He came back with the good news Angela was fine. He reiterated that the hospital was careful and still had her in an incubator because she was underweight. I wanted to see her, so Hossein got me up

and helped me walk to the viewing area. When I saw her, my bubbling emotions and anxiety were quelled. I was finally able to breathe a sigh of relief as a wave of tranquility and stillness washed over me. She was bundled up in a blanket and seemed happy. It is a practice in Iran to wrap a newborn baby tightly in a

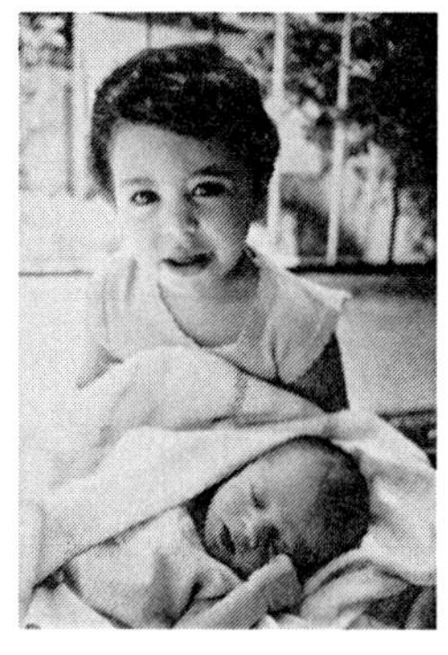

cover so they feel like they are still in the mother's womb.

The doctor wanted Angela to stay in the hospital for a week to make sure she was gaining weight and no other issues occur. That was very hard for me not to have her for a week. The next day Hossein took me home without her. It was very hard to leave her at the hospital, and I wanted to hold her and care for her. I felt so lost, I was searching for that part of me that was missing. Hossein tried to make me feel better but he couldn't give me what I lost.

My breasts started to hurt, they needed to pumped and relieved of the milk, but I needed help. Ava's daughter was still breastfeeding, so she had her latch onto my breasts to try to get the milk flowing. It was hard, and I was not very successful but we kept trying. In the Iranian culture, if another lady helps to breastfeed your baby, she is technical a second mother. So her baby was my baby, too.

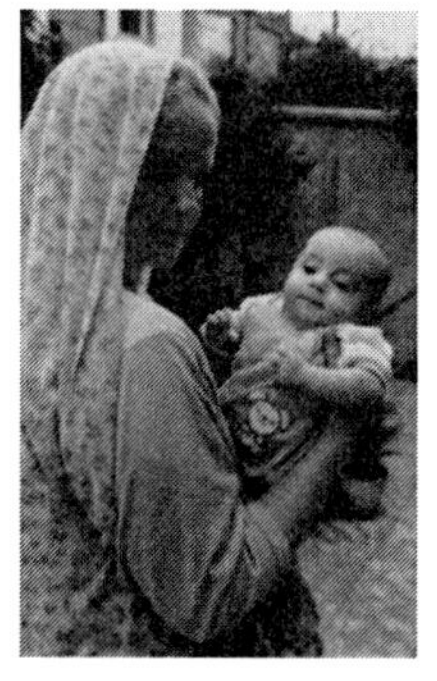

I told Hossein about two days later that I needed to visit Angela. So off we went to visit and check up on her. The hospital staff talked to Hossein about

Angela staying longer than a week. I became very irate. 'Why' was the only word that could come out of my mouth. Hossein could see how flustered I was and told me that we would call the doctor in the morning.

The next morning, when Hossein finished talking to the doctor, he turned to me and said we will go tomorrow and get Angela. She was healthy enough and she did not need to stay longer like the hospital wanted. The doctor would give the order for the hospital to release her. I was relieved that I knew I was getting my baby back. I had hope again, and I felt the cold husk of depression peel away. I wanted to hold my baby so desperately. Mohammad and Hossein drove me to the hospital and I was able to do just that. We did not have special baby car seats in Iran. I sat in the back of the car with a cloth baby carrier. I gave her so many kisses and talked to her, and she smiled back. I got her home and gave her a once over. She was about 17 and ½ inches long at birth and only four pounds in weight. My first duty was to fatten her up. I tried to breastfeed her but she rejected my milk. OK, she had been bottle fed so we would go that route. The next morning, when Hossein finished talking to the doctor, he turned to me and said we will go tomorrow and get Angela. She was healthy enough and she did not need to stay longer like the hospital wanted. The doctor would give the order for the hospital to release her. I was relieved that I knew I was getting my baby back. I had hope again, and I felt the cold husk of depression peel away. I wanted to hold my baby so desperately. Mohammad and Hossein drove me to the hospital and I was able to do just that. We did not have special baby car seats in Iran. I sat in the back of the car with a cloth baby carrier. I gave her so many kisses and talked to her, and she smiled back. I got her home and gave her a once over. She was about 17 and ½ inches long at birth and only four pounds in weight. My first duty was to fatten her up. I tried to breastfeed her but she rejected my milk. OK, she had been bottle fed so we would go that route.

Hossein was able to get some Nestle baby formula and I was feeding her every time she told me she was hungry by being fussy. By the end of the first couple of weeks, she was gaining weight. I did surprise everyone in the family with the way I cared for her. I had a natural instinct for knowing what to do and I did it with courage. My goal was to get her at a healthy weight. But I was also so nervous. I started to lose hair from my head just above my hairline. It looked like I had a hairband on too long and there was a long thin line of my scalp shining through my hair. It did take some time to grow back. It is funny how your body reacts to stress.

7

The Intimate World

Yes, we enjoyed having sex with each other. We were both young and very active in that department. Hossein had a bodybuilder's physique and I certainly enjoyed looking at him. I loved the way that he could move his pecks. He did it at times I was not expecting and would crack me up laughing. I was never skinny but had a healthy body. I was biking and doing a little jogging at the time we first met so I was pretty fit, too. It was easy to let go of my worries when I was with him.

Some interesting things popped up regarding my husband and how Iranians thought about sex. For example, he believed in being clean-shaven in the private area of the body. They thought that hair was not clean. Your skin was not very sexy with hair everywhere. My husband even shaved his back and sometimes I helped him. For such an ancient culture, this might seem odd. Me, being a well-read scholar of dime-store historical romance novels, knew about this fact already.

I was not very up-to-date about the sexual revolution in America. I was shy about my body. Hossein began teaching me how to be more adventurous in my lovemaking. There would be some steamy bedroom scenes in this section, but that's not the kind of book I am writing.

Let me go further along telling you about the Iranian customs of old. I cannot speak for modern-day Iranians; this was all experienced in the 1980s. My husband was more traditional in his hygiene except for showers. He loved taking showers daily like most Americans. Water is a precious commodity in Iran. Some areas like Kashan did not see rain very often. More rain occurred in Tehran, but I rarely saw rain in Kashan. I had an umbrella mostly for the sun.

In Kashan of old, they had hammams in the neighborhood. Some people know them as Turkish or Roman baths. They did not have a shower at home except for washing themselves after the toilet and for prayer via faucet. The women and men would alternate the days they used the bath. The women would sit in small groups and scrub each other's skin to take all the old dry skin off. They would use cold, warm, and hot water at different parts of the process. This would take about four hours. Some women would apply henna, which is a red dye, on their hair, hands, and feet. Unlike other typical henna usage, this did not include designs, and was instead just to tint them red. It was believed it had health benefits. There was also a custom of taking all of the hair off the face, except for eyelashes and eyebrows. It was called threading. I have just recently seen it being done at some of the beauty shops here in America. They get a string and twist it in a way to pull the hair follicle all the way to the root, off the face. I had it done once. I cried because it was so painful. It is like having a bikini wax. They shaped their eyebrows and anything else that needed attention. When they got finished, they did very little for the rest of the day. This bathing ritual was exhausting and felt like running a marathon.

The men's cleaning day is less luxurious, and more of a down to business rough scrub shower. Taking away all of the impurities, most men left the showers like a shucked corn on the cob. They washed themselves on Thursdays, the day right before Friday prayers in the Mosque. The body must be spotless during prayers, as a clean vessel is a holy vessel, which allows your prayers to reach God. This includes everything such as hair, sweat, dirt, and even bodily fluids.

Most traditional Iranian adults had sex about once a week. There is also a shower once a week. Water is precious, so saving water by doing dirty things before the weekly shower makes sense. Therefore, the only reason somebody would need to take daily showers, is if they are constantly getting dirty somehow. So there was a mental connection between cleaning yourself and having sex.

Being an American, taking daily showers was almost expected. It was sweltering hot in Iran and wearing a veil outside made me sweat profusely. The water always felt so good when I got home, I never stopped to think about how I was being perceived. It's funny how such a small cultural difference can mean something so different. Hossein and I must have been having a lot of sex daily for me to be taking so many showers, because I didn't work a dirty job. When this finally came to light, I was simultaneously mortified, while also laughing my head off. They never believed us. They continued teasing us, saying that it was OK to enjoy

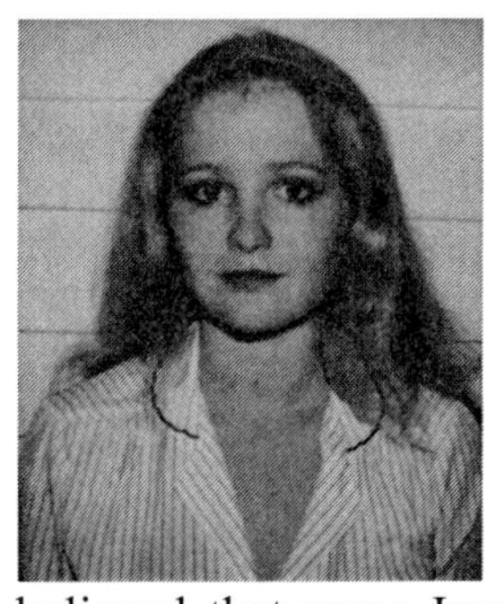

our honeymooning. We could not convince them otherwise. So, we had a reputation of being lovebirds.

American women were known for being promiscuous and inventive in their love-making according to Iranian men. I believed that some Iranian men were jealous of Hossein being married to me. They thought that he had a fabulous sex life. Of course, they did not talk about me but they asked about American women in general to my husband. The Iranian women did talk about sex just like we do in America to each other, but me being an outsider, they found it hard to talk me directly about intimacy. They would occasionally say things in provocative ways to see how I reacted. I think they had this perception that American women were simultaneously more experienced and more tactful about these things.

Speaking on cultural misunderstanding about sex, my husband had an interesting interaction with a soldier at a vehicle checkpoint. We were on a short trip in our American Rambler car, when we were stopped and searched. Hossein was told to open his trunk, and even further, open the briefcase he had in there. Hossein had a picture of me without my veil, in the case. The soldier wanted to know why he had a sexy picture of a blonde lady. Hossein smiled and explained that was his wife and she was seated in the car right now if he did not believe him. The soldier slowly looked into the car and even with my veil on around my face, he noticed my blue eyes. His demeanor changed immediately, from the rough and tumble soldier, to a very apologetic human. He quickly backed away, apologized to Hossein, and waved us to drive on.

My eyes did make me stand out, but that's not always a good thing. One time I was near one of the roundabouts on one of the main streets in Tehran and a couple of men noticed the color of my eyes. I was heading home but I saw that they were following me. I felt scared. I did not know what they wanted from me. I kept a fast pace and went around some other ladies near a veggie stand a few blocks from home. I ducked into the store and acted like I had been there for a while. The shop owner asked what he could do for me and I made eye contact with him and shook my head. Just then, the two guys came running by and looked into the shop. The merchant understood what was happening and asked the guys what they wanted. They brushed him off and left. He watched them go down the street and motioned to me that it was clear to go home. I did not want them to know where I lived for the sake of safety. I was so grateful to him and thanked him profusely. Not everyone had good intentions in any culture. There is always a bad grape or two in a bunch. I got back home and told everyone about my being followed. I wanted them to be aware just in case these guys came around looking for me again. From then on, I wore sunglasses out when I was alone.

8

What is in a Name?

My maiden name is Daniel. I knew that my father's family was from the British Isles. My dad would say that he had a great-grandmother who would only speak Gaelic. Later on, my father did more research and found out that we were descendants of a brother of the founder of Jack Daniel's Brewery Company located in Lynchburg, Tennessee. And the Daniel family came from Wales, Ireland, and maybe Scotland through England. Nothing more significant than that was known in my family tree.

My first name was Roxanne, and I was the first in my family to have this name. My grandmother had a fondness for this name after reading it in a romance novel, and she recommended it to my mother. It was very unique for the area we lived, and I had never met another girl with my name until I went to college. Then a few years later, two songs came out with my name. I loved having random guys come up to me and sing one of the songs.

But the most unusual thing about my name, is the fact that it was originally from Persia. According to legend, Roxanne was a concubine of one of the kings and she ends up marrying Alexander the Great. Roxanne in Persian 65 means the morning light or dawn. Roxanne was pronounced

Roshanak in Farsi. I did not know this until later in life. I did not go looking for someone from that country. It just happened. When I first came to Iran, I thought that having an Iranian name would help me to fit in well. My mother-in-law had other ideas. Since I was coming from a non-Islamic culture, I needed a new name. She wanted me to take the name of Mariam, mother of Jesus. I wanted to be in her good graces so I said it was no problem. I loved my own name and the history behind it, but I bowed to her wishes. Thus, everyone in Iran was introduced to me as Mariam. Roxanne was my past life, even though it was on all of my legal documents.

Hossein's family's name was another interesting story. It was a hyphenated name of Atrchin-Kashi. There was no one else in his country he knew of that had that name. I said Hossein what it meant. He explained.

"In the early 1900s, the people of Iran did not have last names. They were someone who was the son of someone else. The previous Shah made everyone choose a last name. Many people did not know what they should take as a name. Some of the officials recommended using forms of words that had to deal with their occupation. My father-in-law decided to use Atrchin which was a form of the word 'perfume' in his language. It made sense to him since he sold rose water in the bazaar and he was from Kashan. So, he decided to hyphenate his name to Atrchin-Kashi which basically meant perfume dealer from the city of Kashan."

"That is so fascinating. It's very similar to old practices in other countries, such as someone taking the last name Carpenter. But you added a location, so everyone knows what you do and where you are from, just by your name." I replied. This was extremely uncommon, and I never met any Iranian with a similar naming scheme. "Of course, you will have to show me your father's garden where he grew these roses." I finished.

He did get to take me there. The small town of Ghamsar, Iran was not far from Kashan where we lived. It is famous for cultivating Mohammadi roses. Hossein's father had a small garden in Ghamsar. They sold it after Hossein's father died when he was young. It is a lovely oasis of trees and homes in a valley surrounded by desert mountains. It was much cooler there with all of the lovely trees. You could not see the flowers very easily because of the walls surrounding the gardens of rose bushes. We were able to sneak a peek through a couple of open gates, and it was truly an oasis that they cultivated in this dessert valley. In this town, they were famous for making rose water from those petals.

Golab or Rose water is scented water made with rose petals. They believed it to have a lot of naturally good things like vitamins a and c and it has antioxidants that help in reviving dry skin and give it a glowing complexion. It has a number of additional benefits for health, relieving stress and helping with depression to name a few. They believed that rose water is a magic ingredient that can be used for so many different things.

When I was researching the history of rose water, it had been documented to be in use for over 2500 years. It had to have been sold on the Silk Road, too. Out of all rose species, the Iranian red flower, or Mohammedan flower is unique and most botanists have opined that it has been first planted in Iran and then taken to other countries. Since a long time ago, this plant was also used in traditional medicine to treat various diseases including chronic diarrhea, rheumatic pains, blood abnormalities, and sore throat. If you ate sweets or a type of ice cream here, you would probably taste the rose flavor. I would venture to say that they use rose water in Iran more than we use vanilla in America.

If you go to anyone's home, you are offered a shaker of rose water. The host would sprinkle some rose water on your hands, and you would wash your face and hands to freshen up from the journey as you enter their home. If you went to special services at a mosque, they would offer some rose water there. Rose water was the perfume of Iran. I do not know of any other flower's scent that dominates any culture, like roses do in Iran. It was cool to have a name so well-ingrained into Iranian culture. But of course, when we were in America, nobody knew how to pronounce our last name. There was a missing vowel and a rolling Spanish 'r' in the name.

First names were interesting, too. Mohammad is a very common name along with Ali for boys' names. The first son was usually named Mohammad after the founding prophet of Islam. Ali was his son-in-law. Learning about the history of Islam, many of the descendants' names of the prophet Mohammad were used for religious families' children. Just as many children in America are given Biblical names. For a female, Fatima, the daughter of Mohammad was a common name. The Iranians also used ancient historical names of Iranian past kings and notable figures from the past. My mother-in-law gave her sons religious names while my brother-in-law gave his kids' historical names from ancient Persia. It seems that where we draw inspiration for names, is very similar across the world. We all want our names to have meanings and history, and I am blessed to be born a Daniel while gaining the name Atrchin-Kashi.

Next, was the problem of naming my daughter. We had already decided on the name of Angela but the Iranian parliament had decreed that no foreign names would be allowed on birth certificates. I wanted the name to be official. Since we would have Iranian and American passports for her, I thought that it was important that everything had the same pronunciation. Hossein agreed with me. The first place he went to register her birth would not accept this foreign name. He came back home to make a plan.

Being a religious country, they had accepted names like Mary and Moses. We had to make sure that we explained that Angela meant "Angel of God" or "Messenger of God". He went to another place. I had high hopes for our justification of having her name. He came back with still no approval. He tried one last time at an office that was close the International Embassies. He came back with a smile. He had succeeded. Angela's name was official in both languages. I was so happy.

Voice of America and BBC were the only friends on the radio I could listen to every day that gave me a scent of home. There were scarcely any English programs on T.V. The radio kept me sane whenever I was alone. Whenever everyone went to work, I was home with Angela, Hossein's mom, and sometimes my niece. When everyone was taking a nap, I would listen to those two stations. Hossein told me to be careful. We were not supposed to be listening to the foreign broadcast. Music that had female singers were not allowed in Iran. The religious leaders believed that men would think sexually about, as well as covet a woman that was not theirs if they heard her singing.

OK, so I listened very quietly to the radio. Voice of America promoted a utopian view of life in America. It was very disillusioning to see an American radio station try so hard to impress people. It wasn't great but made my life bearable. I got to listen to some of the latest music and singers which kept me up to date. BBC was my favorite broadcast. It felt like it reported on more international news, and tried to present only the facts without political motivation. It also played many different radio dramas, such as Sherlock Holmes short stories. I could sit for hours listening to BBC.

I had unintentionally smuggled some music cassette tapes in with me when I came to Iran. My brother-in-law saw the small collection of tapes in my shipped boxes. The guy who was checking my things to make sure that I did not have anything illegal was opening each container. Mohammad grabbed the tapes and put them under his jacket. He knew that my music was not evil, but security would throw them all away because foreign music was unacceptable in Iran at that moment. Yes, I carried the great evil and sexy artists, such as the heretic John Denver, and the alluring James Taylor. Regardless of how innocuous I thought these musicians to be, it was not permitted in Iran. I smiled and thanked Mohammad for saving them for me.

I was an avid book reader, I brought about twenty books with me to read. Luckily, the airport security did not have a problem with my books. Whenever we would have family gatherings, they would talk about politics and other complicated things. I never understand everything was being said and would get bored very easily. I would get one of my books out, read while sitting with the family, and I would find myself immersed in the story. I read so much, that I reread my stories at least thrice. That bothered Hossein, he said I was being rude. I explained that I was giving him a break to not translate what was being said all the time. I could be with them and occupied at the same time. I think he finally understood my dilemma and didn't bother me about it again.

9

Roaming Around Tehran

I basically stayed in two of the cities of Iran. I was in Tehran for the first six months and then I lived in Kashan for more than three years. Tehran, which is the capital of Iran was huge and difficult to get around. We did not always have a car to drive because my brother-in-law would use it for only long-distance outings. All shopping was done by walking. We womenfolk carried everything home in our hands wearing a chador. Luckily, we had a very small store that carried milk, coke, and some canned foods across the street. There are lots of roundabouts in most of the cities I traveled to. Crossing the major streets was a huge challenge. Nobody obeyed the traffic lights. I have even seen people driving in the wrong direction. If you had to get to the other side of the street, you had to be careful. It was a fine art of weaving through the cars and trucks. I usually held on to my husband's hand or my sister-in-law's chador in crossing these major streets.

We had to walk about a mile to get some flatbread. That is something I loved to do. We would leave the house at about 4 o'clock in the morning, walk that mile and get in line for bread. The way they made the bread was interesting. There was an oven called a tandoor in the ground and another hole for the baker to stand in. The baker would get some really thin dough spread over something that looked like a padded shield. He would hit the shield on the inside of the side of the oven and the dough would stick to the wall. The bread would be done within two minutes. We would

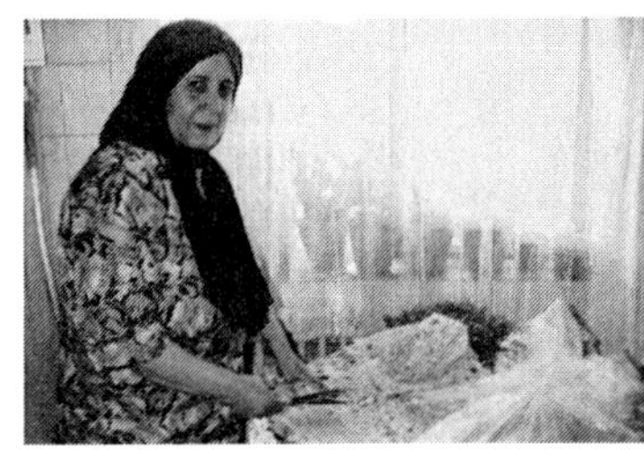

buy the maximum of 20 loaves of bread allowed per customer. As some as we got home, we would put the five or so loaves of bread we would use for the next couple of days in a plastic bag. The rest of the bread would be cut up into smaller squares and laid out on the table to dry like crackers. This would be good to eat with soup and yogurt.

There are different types of flat bread or 'nan' in Farsi. We had very thin flatbread called lavash, a slightly thicker Nan-e taftoon flatbread which was my favorite, as well as the thickest Nan-e-barbari for kabab. Nan-e barbari usually has poppy or sesame seeds sprinkled on it. A fourth flatbread type was Nan-e sangak which was similar in thickness to nan-e-barbari, but made very differently. They cooked this dough over stones, which was a long held tradition. So, when you buy some, you have to double-check to make sure that you are not biting into a stone. I really loved them all but I do love bread. I did not see any

American yeast-made bread near where we lived. I did not see any taco shells or cornmeal. That was OK, though. I enjoyed the different types of flat bread. It is my downfall. Forget the sweets, bread is the king as far as I prefer.

The vegetable stalls were where we would buy our veggies and fruit. We would only buy what was in season and it was limited to what was grown in Iran. Because of the Iran-Iraq war, they did not import specialty foods and veggies. We only had to walk about three blocks to get to these places. There were some clothing stores, material shops, and household item shops nearby, too. The selection was very limited and cheaply made. But regardless, we got our daily exercise. There is a Grand Bazaar in Tehran but it was a long walk and a taxi trip to go there. And of course, you would have to carry anything you brought back home the same way. It was a tedious trip and I would flop into the shower as soon as I got back home.

My sister-in-law was a principal of an elementary school. She let me come with her to her school one day. I got to meet some of the teachers. All of the girls at this school had to wear long coats and pants and a headdress that covered their hair. The older girls wore veils (chadors) on top of these other things. It could get very hot for these girls during the warm months. I was lucky enough to visit in the winter. The classrooms were bare and I did not notice anything on the walls except pictures of the religious leaders of the day. The books they used were paperback and small in size.

My other sister-in-law taught at a university about nursing. I did not visit that place but she kept very busy. My brother-in-law was a civil engineer so of course, they were constantly at their jobs. My mother-in-law since her stroke rarely moved from inside the home. I got to babysit my niece for periods of time before Angela was born. She learned a few English  words while I learned a few words from her. I would play games with my niece and sing English songs to her.

Shirin was my main teacher in Farsi. She was very patient with me because I kept making her repeat the sounds of the words. I got the guttural sound they had for some words like cucumber. My husband would laugh at me and tell me not to say cucumber before I learned the sounds. It sounded like I was saying penis. I practiced a lot with that word because when I went shopping, I would buy cucumbers. I had succeeded and can still pronounce it to this day.

I did have problems with my rolling Rs though. It is very similar to Spanish but I never did conquer that hill. Another thing I was trying to say was 'good night' and it came out as 'good heaven.' All of the family loved this accidental expression I had created. I guess that I was creating expressions as Hossein did with the English language. It made us all smile and laugh. Seeing each other's customs in different ways helps us to grow.

We would travel around Tehran and go to some of the Shah's old palaces and some museums. The people in charge explained the Shah lived in such exquisite luxury while the poor people in his country starved. Isn't that pretty much the same for kings in countries around the world I thought to myself. The Shah did not build these palaces. He inherited them. They were grand to look at but I was not very impressed. I had not learned to appreciate the fine details of the craftsmanship in every crevice of the palaces yet.

There was even a small zoo in Tehran. The kids loved to see the animals but when we were able to get the kids up on an elephant, Angela protested quite loudly. Luckily, the zoo was not very big. I could not see how they could take care of many animals when they were still in the middle of a war.

Azadi Tower was very interesting to me. It was a modern arch-shaped building constructed in 1971 to commemorate the 2,500th anniversary of the Persian monarchy. It became a symbol of freedom after the 1979 revolution and the name of the tower changed from Shahyad (Kings Memorial) to Azadi (Freedom). I saw this monument the very first day I came to Iran. It was only about 4 miles from where we lived but we had not had the time to go to it until later on in the first year I was there. It was located in a huge roundabout with a lot of cars going around it. We started to cross but Shirin told us that there was an underground route we could go without challenging the cars to get across. It was a very pretty tower and I marveled at its design of the tower. I had never seen a tower like this one. It was very unique. We went up the tower by elevator. It reminded me of the Washington Monument in Washington, D.C. We could see all around Tehran. It was impressive.

There were some very pretty parks that were lush and very green with trees and running water. One park was named La'leh Park (Tulip Park). We would sometimes take some food and have a picnic in these parks with the kids. They were elated in climbing the different playground apparatuses. Having these parks was very nice. It was a break from the war and it made things feel normal. Walking among the flowers and watching kids play transported me back to the parks in America. I felt like I was home.

There were many grand mosques in Tehran, but I focused on the ones in Kashan, Isfahan, and Shiraz. Tehran was too busy to have an enjoyable moment of solitude in a mosque. I did get to visit an Armenian Christian church named Saint Sarkis Cathedral built in 1971 in Tehran. I was not familiar with this Saint and had to do a little research. I understood that this saint was a general in the Roman army stationed in Turkey and converted to Christianity. He went into exile in Persia during the reign of the pagan Roman emperor Julian. I was quite impressed with the size and design of the church. It stood out from all of the other buildings around it.

We traveled to the north of Tehran going up Vali-e-Asr Ave. This area was very mountainous and not far from Mt. Damavand which is the highest mountain in Iran and the

highest inactive volcano in Asia. Every time we went into this area, it was mostly misty and I could never get a close-up picture of the mountain. This area was nicer than the main city. I even saw a guy with a horse and he let people ride for a

small fee. I wanted to get Angela on a horse. Mohammed was afraid and Hossein explained to him that my family use to own horses and I had taken horseback riding lessons. I got Angela up in front of me and got Nahid right behind and we walked and trotted around a little. I think that Mohammed was surprised at me knowing this. I was a typical cowgirl from Texas as I would explain to Mohammed. I spent a lot of time around animals. I even owned a pony named Nugget for several years when I was young. It was hard for me to be afraid of any animal.

Eventually, my brother-in-law brought some property up in this northern part of Tehran near Tajesh Square and built a medium size apartment building for his family and kids to have for their future. He let me look at his blueprints and I mentioned that the kitchen for such a large apartment was small. I knew that in America kitchens were evolving into the main family meeting place. He reconsidered his design and enlarged the kitchen on my suggestion. I thought that it was cool that he took my advice.

Of the two cities that I lived in, Tehran was very dirty and almost ugly. I did not see very many nice buildings. It reminded me of the Russian plain block buildings that were so unimpressive to look at. Only the old buildings in the city had any personality. It was like a wave of gloom had settled on this modern city. I have not been to Iran recently but I have seen some newer construction and buildings being built and shown on YouTube. It gives me hope for Tehran.

10

Roaming Around Kashan

I think that my favorite place to visit or live was in Kashan. It was so much quieter when I visited local mosques and old house museums here. Kashan was once considered one of the most prosperous oases in Iran. The word Kashi is derived from city's naming meaning tiles. Kashan is known for its tilework, carpets, silk, and other textiles. Rose water is also produced in the area. It was also thought to be home to at least one of the three wise kings who visited Jesus when he was born. It was even mentioned in some of my research that the Mongol forces of Genghis Khan besieged this city and many stayed. Kashan is located about hundred and fifty miles south of the capital of Tehran. It is located between the Dasht-e Kavir (salt desert) on the east and the Zagros mountains to the west.

My all-time favorite place was the Kashan bazaar. It was a lot closer to our house than the bazaar in Tehran. It required only one taxi or mini-bus to hop on and drive about 10 minutes to get there from my home. I also learned to negotiate the price of traveling before I get in the vehicle. The drivers will double the price if you do not discuss this issue first. And of course, there were no safety belts.

Shirin introduced me to this amazing bazaar for the first time. It was a maze of small covered alleys going in different directions. I was so interested in all of the different stores that we went to. I did not pay attention to the direction we were going and I was easily lost. I usually had a good sense of direction, but in this labyrinth thank God, Shirin knew where to go.

There were sections for each item you would buy. It was like trade guilds were set up. There were spice areas, material shops, carpet merchants, metal shops making pots and pans by hand, cheap plastic things for the house, and so much more that I can't list it all. The carpet sellers had the most upscale shops. I think that they had been established in this part of the bazaar for a long time. This area felt old like a beautiful woman aging gracefully. It seemed like the merchants did very little work at all. They just sat around, drank tea, and discussed the happenings of the day. Occasionally someone would come in to look at a rug. I just could not understand how they were able to stay in business that way.

In the different alleys, you could find beautiful small mosques to pray in. There were fountains to wash their hands for prayers. There were madrassahs (religious schools) and caravanserais (places where long ago travelers could spend the night) throughout the bazaar. The long corridors of vaulted ceilings were so bewitching. The elaborate brick patterns in the ceilings with a circle of light streaming through from the outside illuminated the rooms. I could sit for hours looking at it all. It was a very noisy place in some parts of the bazaar, especially for the people bartering and the pounding of metal from the pot-makers.

They had a rhythm of sounds. I also loved going into the quiet area of the mosque just outside of the main passageway. It was very calming to me. It would give me time to reflect on what I had seen.

You were expected to barter in the bazaar when you shopped. There was a list price but you did not pay it. You would ask how much. You did not want to be too interested in something or they would jack up the price. Shirin told me to cover myself really well so they did not know that a foreigner was with her so she could get a better deal. Being foreign drove up the prices but not very many foreigners came to Kashan. They were not expecting me to be a foreigner wearing a chador.

Whatever the list price was, you would protest and say they were crazy to charge that much. This item is not worth that of a price. You would counter back with less than half of the price they stated. They would say no, they could not make a living selling it that cheaply. It goes back and forth until a price is agreed upon. Sometimes we would have to actually walk away before the merchant would lower his price. It was definitely a game that everyone played. Sometimes you would agree to a price, the merchant would bag it up and you only gave a part of the money that had been agreed to. Sometimes the merchant would laugh, break down and give the item to you. Sometimes they would hold their hand out until you gave them the full agreed price. Iranians are like this in a lot of their dealings. They expect people to barter for something if it is important. I guess that this was why the silk road came through this area. The merchants knew how to persuade caravans to deal with them.

There is also Taarof which is another form of their culture, which is almost the opposite of haggling. It is a polite way of saying "It is free for you." or "It is my pleasure to give it to you." Most of the time the merchant really needed the money, but were just being benevolent. You usually have to insist on paying him, usually several times, until they will accept the money. I found this problem happening to me all of the time. Once they found out that I was a foreigner living in their country, they wanted to honor me and show how polite and generous they were. Friends and people you meet will go out of their way to be polite to you. If you are eating at a restaurant with them, they will insist on paying for the meal. I had to go to the owner to pay ahead of time if I wanted to pay for my friends.

I did a little research on the history of the Kashan bazaar. It was believed to have been founded in the Seljuk period around the tenth century but some locals believe that it is much older. The architecture is phenomenal in the Timche-ye Amin od-Dowleh section where a well was built. There are also tombs, baths, plazas, and water reservoirs built at different periods. Once I learned about going around the bazaar, the merchants got to know me a little more and knew that I was officially a local. That was nice. They did not try to charge me more and I developed the art of bargaining.

Remember that everything we paid for, we had to carry home by hand. For any shopping in Kashan we had to do, we needed to take a bus or taxi. In Iran, most taxis would ferry up to 5 people in a rideshare style capacity. Two would sit up next to the driver since 3 would be in the backseats. The taxi was constantly picking up and

dropping off passengers at different places. The 1967 American Rambler, gifted to Hossein by his brother, only got used once or twice a month. We used it mainly for if we needed to buy meat which needed to be taken home quickly or when we had large or heavy items like appliances that we needed to bring home. The car was also used for traveling longer distances outside of town. Gasoline was not expensive, but there were no gas stations anywhere. At some points during the Iran–Iraq war, gasoline was rationed like other goods. My other family members handled the ration cards for me that we were issued for the war efforts. Either my husband or my sister-in-law would make sure we got our fair share of rice and other commodities that were in short supply during this time.

Hossein would drive around the town and show me the older part of Kashan. I loved it. There was a fragment of an ancient wall around the town still standing. At the time of writing this, this mudbrick rampart is being restored. There was this cool-looking building that was shaped like a pointed dome. Hossein explained that it was a very old refrigeration building to keep ice cool during the summer. It was no longer in use except for storage. Most of these things were built around the eleventh century. As we were discussing this building, an old farmer was walking by. He had with him a donkey with a few things packed on the back. I asked the farmer if I could get a picture of Hossein next to the donkey with Angela sitting on the back. The farmer said sure, but the donkey may not like it. I was used to being around animals like horses. I explained that we would do it quickly. I encouraged Hossein to place Angela on its back. The donkey turned its head to try to bite Hossein, and he

leaped back so fast with Angela in his arms, that the farmer and I burst into laughter. The visual of a herculean figure wielding a small child like a shield from the evil hydra-donkey was hilarious. After I had composed myself, I went to the donkey, grabbed the reins, and kept the donkey's head away from Hossein while he placed Angela on its back. I was able to get the picture, and capture the moment perfectly. Notably the picture in this chapter is of him being a little scaredy-cat. I teased Hossein after that so much. I would point to something behind him and yell donkey. Instantly, he jumped and turned to see nothing. Laughter ensued. Hossein would drive around the town and show me the older part of Kashan. I loved it. There was a fragment of an ancient wall around the town still standing. At the time of writing this, this mudbrick rampart is being restored. There was this cool-looking building that was shaped like a pointed dome. Hossein explained that it was a very old refrigeration building to keep ice cool during the summer. It was no longer in use except for storage. Most of these things were built around the eleventh century. As we were discussing this building, an old farmer was walking by. He had with him a donkey with a few things packed on the back. I asked the farmer if I could get a picture of Hossein next to the donkey with Angela sitting on the back. The farmer said sure, but the donkey may not like it. I was used to being around animals like horses. I explained that we would do it quickly. I encouraged Hossein to place Angela on its back. The donkey turned its head to try to bite Hossein, and he leaped back so fast with Angela in his arms, that the farmer and I burst into laughter. The visual of a herculean figure wielding a small child like a shield from the evil hydra-donkey was hilarious. After I had composed myself, I went to the donkey, grabbed the reins, and kept the donkey's head away from Hossein while he placed Angela on its back. I was able to get the picture, and capture the moment perfectly. Notably the picture in this chapter is of him being a little scaredy-cat. I teased Hossein after that so much. I would point to something behind him and yell donkey. Instantly, he jumped and turned to see nothing. Laughter ensued.

I noticed on the top of some of the older buildings, they had these types of chimney-looking things. Hossein explained that they were wind vents (badgirs) to catch the wind and funnel the air down into the building to cool it down. The air-conditioning unit they have in the newer buildings does not work very well so, in summer, we did not go out from about 11 a.m. to about 5 p.m. The bazaar even closed down. So, most people did their shopping early morning and late evening. The temperature during the summer stayed in the upper 90s to upper 100s with no rain. I used my umbrella for protection from the sun. Although we did have snow one winter.

The older homes in Kashan were very unique. These houses were C shaped, with a courtyard in the front. The mud walls surrounded the entire house including said courtyard, which allowed many families to safely keep belongings outside while still retaining privacy. The only door to the house opened at the courtyard, which was effectively the houses front door. There was a special door knocker for women and one for men to let the person inside know what sex was outside their door. The knocker had different sounds. The one that was more like a circle was the females' and the males' knocker hung down like a penis. After you were greeted, you would go into the courtyard leading to the main building. A lot of entertaining was done in the courtyard during the cooler evening hours. Even dinner would be served there.

Of all of the mosques and shrines in the area, one of my favorites to visit was Agha Bozorg Mosque. The translation of Agha Bozorg means Mister Big. It was built in the eighteenth century. There were other mosques and holy shrines peppered throughout the area like Masjid Jami (Friday Mosque), Boq'eh Shahzadeh Ibrahim, Boq'eh Baba Afzal, and Masjid Vazir dating from the sixth century all

the way up to the nineteenth century. And for a side note, there are a lot of Mosques in different cities with the name Jami (or Friday). They emphasizing the fact that It's called Friday mosque because you go on Fridays. It is like naming one of our churches in most major cities 'Sunday Church.'

We lived on a street called Amir Kebir, and just up the road there was also a place called Fin Garden. It was a beautiful place full of old cypress trees. An old name of the gardens used to be Shah's garden but when regimes changes, places named after them are discarded and replaced. This garden completed in 1590 (during the Safavid period) is one of the oldest gardens in Iran and is a

UNESCO World Heritage site. It has a sad history of having a famous chancellor murdered in the bath area of the garden. However, it was still a tranquil and awe-inspiring place for me to roam around in. There is a stream of mountain water coming down a long canal of small fountains.

I would cool my feet in the water. The large pool of water at the center of the garden was where I spent most of my time. Goldish were thriving in the cold clear mountain water, and this not being their natural habitat, leads me to believe someone placed them there. It was so serene sitting and watching my daughter play.

11

Traveling Back from Tehran to Kashan

After about four months after delivering my daughter, we moved to Kashan for Hossein's job. He became a manager in a Kashan Carpet factory. The carpets were machine-made but of very nice quality. Because we were living about 150 miles apart, we had to travel about once a month to see his family. He could not find a job in Tehran because of me.

So, Hossein was hired in the city of Kashan at the Kashan Macmil factory. His family was originally from Kashan and many people knew the family. This city sits in the province of Isfahan pretty much in the center of Iran. It sits on the edge of the Maranjab Desert. The desert does have sand dunes but I did not get to venture into that part of it. I saw a lot of sagebrush types of desert similar to what I was used to in the western part of Texas where my family had lived for a spell. It was beautiful to me. I loved the cactus flowers and wild little lizards moving all around.

The geology of Iran is very different from the area of Georgia in the United States where I was last living. The average height of the land is about 3,300 ft above sea level. It is said that it is shaped like a bowl with tall mountains surrounding it. Sixty percent of it is either arid or semi-arid. Near the Caspian Sea to the north, you can find juniper, elm, beech, and oak forests. It has a salt desert (Dasht-e-Kavir) and a sand desert (Dasht-e-Lut). It is located in an active earthquake zone. The one main Karun River runs 528 miles from the Zagros Mountains and joins up with the Arvan-rud in Khoran Shahr. Most Iranian rivers are not permanent and never reach the sea. Zayande-rud in Isfahan ends up in the Ghavkhaneh marshes. Irrigation is a must for most of Iran. Luckily the mountains are tall enough to collect snow.

According to the 2006 census, there are about 70 million people with many ethnic groups like the Kurds, Lurs, Bakhtiaris, and Boluchs living in and around the mountains. Along with the majority of Muslims, there are religious minorities of Zoroastrians, Jews, Christians, and Baha'i. Iranian officials were not very kind to the Baha'is. They are the only minority that does not have constitutional protection. According to Iranian law, Baha'is have no protection against assault, killings, or other forms of persecution which is very sad. Iran is not perfect in how they deal with some of its people.

In our travels back and forth from Kashan to Tehran, I could see a salty lake named Namak Lake or Dasht-e-Kavir. It was the bed of an extinct interior sea and is considered to be one of the aridest depressions in the world. It looked so big. When we drove passed it, I could look in the distance at the searing heat raising from the salty sand like a mirage. It was an

enduring battle between water and survival out there. There were no roads to it from the highway we drove on so I was not able to get closer to it.

This route was part of one of the parts of the ordinal Silk Road. They had caravanserais stretched about every 25 miles for the caravans of camels and goods to stay at for the night. Merchants needed protection from thieves along the road. One of those places near the highway to Qum is called Caravasera Pasagan. It can bring you way back into the thirteenth century and you can imagine the camels coming into the building to be cooled off from the dry heat and corrosive desert wind of the trip. The recesses in the adobe walls of the building were big enough to be havens of shadows from the heat of the day. To escape from the direct heat of the sun was marvelous.

I also spotted a fire temple named Niasar fire Temple or Chahar Bagh. My brother-in-law Mohammed was with us and I talked them into stopping near the base of the small rocky mountain. It didn't seem too far up to climb so I challenged the guys to climb with me up. Boy, was I wrong?

I had sandals on and we had Angela who at that time was about eight months old. Hossein handed me the baby because he was having problems climbing. I was laughing too much at these two guys that could not climb very well. I got up a little farer and noticed that the rocks were not the best to climb on and the distance was farther than I thought. I turned and said that I think that this was too much of a challenge with a kid in tow. They happily agreed. I learned later that there was a very bumpy road on the other side of the mountain we could have taken.

On one side of the highway, we had the desert, but on the other side in the far distance, I could see mountains. I knew that there were two mountain ranges in Iran. One was to the north of Tehran named the Alborz Range in which the most prodigious Mt. Damavand was the highest with an elevation of 18,600 ft. The other one was named the Zagros Range in the western part of Iran. These mountains were most definitely on the west side of the highway. Another part of that chain of mountains was the Karkas (which means vulture) Mountains. There was one beautiful mountain that stood out above the clouds. At first thought, I would have sworn that it was Mt. Damavand but the location would be all wrong. That mountain was about 92 miles away. It could possibly be the Karkas summit which rises to an elevation of 3,895 miles. A great geographer from the eighth century named Hamdollah Mostowfi describes the mountain as, "A great and high mountain, which a vulture cannot fly upon it because of its height." I do not know if I will ever find out for sure. Most of the locals I asked did not know either.

We traveled through the outskirts of Qum to get back to Kashan. Qum is a famous religious city in Iran. There was a checkpoint there with army personnel checking who was traveling on the highway. Hossein would show his id and we were on our way. They never bothered me but I was veiled. They could not tell that I was a foreigner. A couple of times we went into the city. I was able to visit the Fatima Masumeh Shrine there. It was a smaller shrine but very pretty. It is dedicated to the sister of the eighth Iman Reza who is buried in Mashhad. According to Shia Islam, women if they are close relatives to one of the Twelver Imams were often revered as saints. The shrine was built around the seventh century.

Qum is also famous for a flat sweet type of cookie made from sweet flour, clarified butter, almonds, cardamon paste, pistachios, and saffron. It is called Sohan. My brother-in-law had a favorite store he would go and buy from whenever he was in that city. Another sweet nougat made with tamarisk manna was also available called gaz. You can buy both of these in Iranian stores in America. They do taste pretty good. Try them if you are able to find a store that sells them.

Coming into Kashan the road has pine trees along the route. They were planted there to protect the road from developing sand dunes and also the road looks nicer with the little bit of contrast of the flat desert land. You could see the Karras mountains in the distance.

I do have a side story to tell about the pine trees. One year in Kashan, I wanted to create a Christmas for Angela and the neighborhood children. I asked Hossein how we could get a tree. A pine tree would be the best. Hossein thought for a while. He told me and a neighbor friend of his to bring a saw and we were going tree hunting. Yes, you guessed it. We went to the road coming into Kashan where all of the pine trees were. It was late in the evening. I did not think that we would have permission to cut one down. Trees were scarce in that part of Iran. Hossein was being his own usual self. He was having a lot of fun on this Christmas tree mission. Most of the trees were bigger when we needed them. I just wanted one about six to seven feet tall. He found one. Now this time of night, the highway was not too busy. Hossein and his friend got to sawing the small tree. Every time a car would come by, he acted like he had to pee. It was so funny how they acted like scared rabbits in car lights.

They were able to cut the tree down. Luckily the tree we cut down was nestled behind a few other trees, so I doubt if anyone ever missed it. We threw a small soiree and told all the local kids families we knew to come help decorate. Upwards of 20 kids came and joyously decorated the tree. The tree's sacrifice was well honored by all who partook in the festivities. We strung popcorn strings and put fabric bows on the tree. I got creative and found a way to replicate Christmas ornaments. I sucked out some egg yolks by putting a small hole on each end of the egg, which we then washed and painted. I glued a string to the top and we hung them on the tree.

In Islam, Jesus Christ was a holy prophet (not the son of God) and they do honor him. The families in our neighborhood came by after the tree was decorated and joined in on our celebration. The kids took many pictures with themselves in front of the tree.

I also want to repeat that it is also a belief that one of the three wise men that went to Bethlehem was from Kashan. It was Melchior from Iran, Gaspar from India, and Balthazar from Arabia according to the legend. So many Kashanies loved the story of the birth of Christ.

12

Food Experiences
the Good and the Bad

I had some unusual times in Iran with food and drink. This chapter is devoted to those experiences. To prepare anyone who is coming to Iran to visit, I think of Montezuma's revenge. Most Americans understand not to drink the water in Mexico. I can attest that the same time happens in Iran. The bathroom and I became good friends.

My husband and I had to go and get my daughter registered with the American interest section at the Swiss Embassy. I wanted to get her an American passport. I had to prove that I had lived in America for at least 10 years. Luckily, I had brought all of my personal papers with me. My high school transcript, job recommendations, and my college transcript.

The lady at the Embassy was surprised that I had not checked in with them sooner to state that I was in the country. I didn't need anything from them and they could not do anything for me. Once you leave your country and go to another place that does not have an American Consulate in it, you are already taking your life into your own hands.

Hossein took me into an area that served some foreign foods near the embassy. I was a little homesick for American food. This one store had turkey and dressing the way we made turkey for Thanksgiving. I was missing tacos, cheddar cheese, and many other foods from home that they did not have or were too expensive to buy. So, we ordered some of the turkey and fixings and sat down at a table to eat. It was delicious. By the time we got back home my stomach was creating all sorts of sounds. I threw up about an hour later and had constant diarrhea for the next two days.

I was dehydrated and weak. I must have had food poisoning. Shirin fussed at Hossein for letting me eat out like that. She was very good at making food for me and making sure that everything was cooked well. She insisted when she brought meat from the butchers that it had to be fresh. After about 3 days, I was actually getting hungry. She wanted to make me some chicken soup. She believed that it would give me some energy. She sounded just like our grandmothers and mothers here in the states. Chicken soup is the savior of the world when it came down to making sick people feel better.

She called for me to come, sit down and eat some of this life-saving soup. I was still weak but wanted some food. She spooned out some of the soup into a bowl and handed it to me. I saw some vegetables and they had a good smell. I put my spoon into the soup and a chicken's head floated to the top of the bowl. I looked at it in disbelief. It was a rooster's head with the comb still attached to it. The eyeballs were staring at me.

I turned to look at her. She explained that the chicken's head had extra nutrients and that eating the eyes would give me extra energy. I apologized that I was not going to be able to eat the soup. I was so happy that I had not thrown up. I did not have anything in my belly to do so. She did not know that chicken heads in our foods in America were not a common occurrence. I did eventually get better and started to eat again. Shirin learned to not to give me chicken heads in my soup in the future. All I can tell you now is I will never be able to look at chicken soup normally anymore. My thoughts will go back to that rooster's head floating in the soup again.

I fell in love with the old pots and pans of Iran. They were different from what we had in America. Non-stick pans were not common at this time. Most of their cooking utensils were heavy. They utilized a lot of large metal platters to serve rice. They had a number of various sizes of bowls for their stews. But the cooking wares were made more for an open fire type of cooking. I noticed that in the bazaar, they have miniature versions of these cooking vessels for children's play toys. I started a quest to collect them. These things were all handmade and hammered in the bazaar. They would normally make the items covered in white covering which is like putting a silver glaze on them.

I did not want that added whiting. I loved the rustic look.

Some of the street foods were different from what we are used to. We would have hot dogs and tacos, they have boiled walnuts and boiled fava beans. They will cook corn on the cob over coals and beets would be steaming on sticks. Kabob is quite common on the streets eaten with flatbread.

A common drink they had is yogurt-based water called ub-dugh. They would add salt and mint flavoring. It was the second most popular drink after hot tea. They did have lemonade and soft drinks but were not as common as the top two drinks. Beer and acholic beverages were illegal at this time, although I am sure that if I wanted some, some would be found.

Vegetables and fruits were seasonal. I made a root cellar out of one of our rooms to store vegetables into the winter. Monir shows me how to spread out the potatoes and check constantly for rotting ones. Eat anything that was getting soft. I learned how to make tomato sauce and a type of catsup. Food in Iran could very sweet or sour. Hot, spicy food was not the norm. I learned to cook with sour-dried limes, sour cherries, sour grapes, plums, and barberries. I learned to boil my milk before drinking and hang up yogurt in a cheesecloth bag to drain the extra water and add salt. They do not eat sweet yogurt here in Iran. I learned how to use grape leaves, cook different types of lentils and beans, and how make many types of rice dishes. They were very proud of the long-grain rice they used. Some of the rice even smelt bacon when cooking it. Some areas of Iran like Tabriz were famous for the huge meatballs (Kufteh Tabrizi) they made. Eggs were served for most meals. One of my favorite egg dishes was Sabzi Kuku which consists of eggs with parsley, dill, basil, spinach, and romaine lettuce. They used our spices more like our vegetable plates. Iranian meals typically consisted of rice and a large serving of stew that was jam-packed with spices and seasoning. In comparison the average American meal consisted of a main entrée and side dishes. Rather than having variety of sides, the Iranian stews were the main focus.

They did not have pork or pork products for purchase in this country. We used a lot of walnuts, watermelon seeds, pumpkin seeds, and pistachios. Pecans and peanuts were very expensive and were imported. I learned how to make Iranian torshi (sour vegetables with garlic and cider vinegar). Some of the pickled garlic was so strong, I threatened my husband that he would not get a kiss from me for weeks if he ate any of those things. I got good at drying herbs and making packets of mixed greens to put in the freezer (yes, I had a freezer) for the winter. I felt like I was becoming a pioneer wife in the wild west.

The desserts are not my favorite. They use chickpeas for a lot of their types of sweets which make the sweets very chalky in taste. Rose water is added to a lot of desserts like ice cream and Faloodeh (a type of noodle ice cream). One of the better deserts was Sholezard. It is a type of rice pudding with saffron and of course, rose water. I felt like I was dishonoring my husband's family by not liking the addition of rose flavoring to so many things. It was something I was not used to and it was hard to find a dessert without that rose water taste. To me, it is a bitter taste by itself. I ended up adding lemon juice to whatever had it to cover the taste. This contrariety of sweet and bitter, is present not only in the desserts, but also my experiences there. For every bit of bitter, a symphony of sweets awaited me in this Persian Playground.

I did enjoy the various kababs and many of the stews they made. Abgoosht is a liquid stew of mutton, onions, chickpeas, and dried limes. I loved dipping my flatbreads into this soupy mess of flavor. My mouth is watering now just thinking about tasting it. Another one of my favorites is kask badenjan which was a dry yogurt or whey paste stirred into fried mashed-up eggplant, olive oil, and mint. I did miss the different cheeses we had at home. The only type of cheese we had in Iran was either goat or sheep cheese. Different types of feta cheese were served with flatbread, greens, tomatoes, cucumbers, and walnuts for a normal breakfast. I developed a likeness to this type of breakfast and will still eat it today if I can find the right ingredients. My sister-in-law Ava would also make me some Haleem. It was very similar to oatmeal but with meat and cinnamon (delicious).

All water I drank had to be boiled. I would get sick with the regular tap water. But even then, I did not like the salty taste of Kashan water. Every time we visited Tehran, I would bring gallon containers to fill up and take back down to Kashan to drink. I never realized how different waters can taste from region to region. When I lived in west Texas, the water was similar to the water of Kashan which was very salty.

I had to have a meat grinder for hamburger meat. Shirin taught me how to cut up half of a sheep. She showed me how to add fat to the meat cuts in the grinder to make the meat flavorful when cooking. I would grind the meat three times while adding cut-up onions and seasonings. We usually had sheep meat and sometimes we would get a goat. I loved the sheep meat but the goat meat was a little strong for my tastebuds. Ever since the chicken soup incident, I could not deal with whole chickens and cleaning them.

Hossein would have to buy them already cleaned if I wanted to cook with chicken. We did not have chicken very often. I had a little bit of camel meat but it was very tough. Cow meat was not good in this area. Most animals had worms and we had to be careful to cook all of our foods very well.

When Angela got old enough to go to the toilet by herself, I would help her clean herself as most moms do. I noticed that her stool had a little movement one day. I had Hossein come and look. He says it was tapeworms. We immediately took her to see a doctor. He gave us a series of pills for her to take to get rid of it. I was very attentive every time she went to the restroom. About a day later, a wad of worms the size of a golf ball came out of her. That was the end of that problem, but I learned to cook everything very well. I did not know if this problem came from a cow but I did not want any more cow meat.

In my house months later, my sister-in-law and husband decided that they wanted to make Kaleh pacheh. I will explain later what that is. I was very lucky to have a sister-in-law that could teach me Iranian cooking. I was limited in my southern cooking skills because my mother did not have the patience to teach me without giving up and just cooked on her own. My sister-in-law was very patience so I think that I am better at cooking Iranian food than American food now because of her tutoring me.

My husband had told me about how Iranians like to use all of the parts of an animal and waste nothing. I know that was a practice in old American farming families. The family and neighbors would get together to kill a hog. An old bathtub would be set up in the back near the barn. They would kill the hog, put it into the tub, and use every part. Nothing was wasted.

Well, the same practice occurred here in Iran but with sheep. My husband procured some sheep intestines and tripe for breakfast one morning and attempted to serve me some. I looked at it, smelled it, and politely said no. My sister and brother-in-law were very happy to join him for some of it. Even my daughter liked it.

When my sister-in-law Shirin came to visit from Tehran, we went to the bazaar to do a little shopping. I always love going to the that maze-like shopping center. We paid for some spices for cooking as well as some material to make Angela an outfit. On the way out, we stopped by the butcher. Shirin wanted a sheep's head. "Why? I asked?" She tried to explain to me how delicious it was and she would show me how to cook it. I was not sure how to explain to her that I would not be able to do this endeavor, but I tried to be polite. She knew that I had problems with eating certain parts of animals because of the chicken head experience. She laughed at me and proceeded in buying the head, eyeballs, teeth, and all. The butcher popped it into a plastic bag and we were set to go home.

I knew that I would never eat any part of this sheep's head but I was interested in how she prepared it. She took the sheep's head to the backyard and began to clean it. She got a flame and burned off all the hair around the sheep's face. Then she got a knife and poked it into the ear area and mouth. Talk about looking gross, I asked her what she was doing. She turned and showed me some larva worms that were in the holes. "Oh, my god," I exclaimed. I left her in the yard to continue the surgery on her own.

At that point, there was no way I was tasting any of this special meal. When Hossein got home from work, him and Shirin got to work in the kitchen with the head. They placed it into an Iranian-style pressure cooker, put it on the stove, and started to cook it. I told my husband I was staying away from this meal they were working on. He just laughed and said how good it would be to eat the brains and eyeballs. EW!!

About an hour later, we heard a loud noise in the kitchen like a small bomb had gone off. Luckily not of us was in the kitchen at that time. We looked into the kitchen and the lid of the pressure cooker had exploded off the container. There were sheep brains, pieces of skull bones, and eyeballs everywhere on the 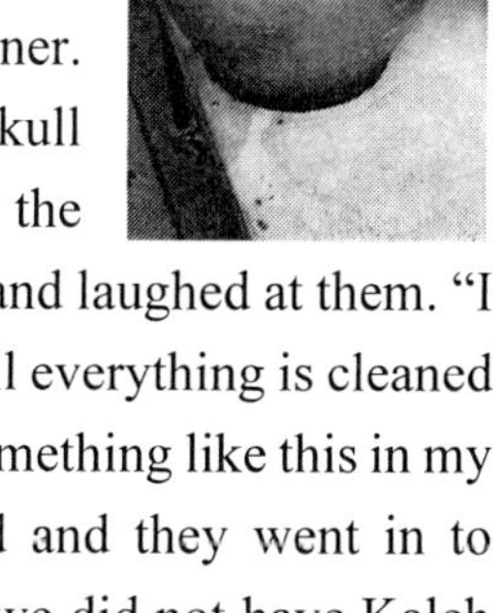 floor, cabinets, and ceiling. I turned and laughed at them. "I am not stepping into that kitchen until everything is cleaned up. Serves you right to be cooking something like this in my Amcrican kitchcn." We all laughed and they went in to clean up the mess. Needless to say, we did not have Kaleh pacheh (sheep's head) that evening for dinner.

13
Villages and Flood Waters

When I was living in Kashan, I used an umbrella hardly ever for rain. I used umbrellas only for the sun. It was a desert environment and it brought back fond memories of when I lived in the desert area of El Paso, Texas with my family when I was young. We were traveling through the desert to villages nearer to the mountain outside of Kashan. My husband's cousin had a summer villa in a very small village in this area. It was lovely. Most villas (our word for a very small home in an isolated spot) had a wall around them made of mud and straw. There was a main room with no furniture, but plenty of carpets to sit on and entertain the guests. There was also a toilet, a kitchen, and a few guest sleeping rooms. We slept on the floor on rolled mattresses and pillows.

I went into the room where all of the women were and sat down on the carpeted floor. We had cushions to lean against. The ladies would talk and drink tea. They would put a sugar cube into their mouths and suck on the sugar while they drank the tea. Some fruit offered along with some sweets and dates. I noticed that cucumbers were treated like a fruit. They peeled and salted it like a banana. I was introduced and one or two of them would test their

English skills on me. Being a newbie and had not gotten far in learning Faris. I could say a few greetings and niceties but not much more. It was very interesting, to say the least, to see only females together while the men gathered next door in another house to talk.

After all of the guests had left, I was able to go into the backyard area. Hossein's cousin had a well that was fed from spring waters from an underground stream. She asked me if I wanted to get into the water which was about four feet deep. The weather was so dry and hot outside, I said yes with great enthusiasm. No one could see us because of the high walls. I jumped in with enthusiasm. The water was freezing but felt so good on my skin.

Let me explain the underground streams. It hardly ever rains in this part of Iran. Snow from the mountains in the far distance creates streams of water. The Iranians of long ago (possibly 3,000 years ago) dug out tunnels deep in the ground to channel the streams to where they needed water. They could be 30 to 130 ft in depth. They maintained using a series of regularly spaced vertical shafts located about every 30 ft or so. These channels of water are called qanats. They are able to capture the much-needed liquid from the water aquifers under the foothills of the mountains and carry the precious cargo to the plains to quench the thirst of the crops and local inhabitants.

My husband and I were lucky enough to see a couple of guys servicing one of these shafts. One guy would lower another one down the shaft on a rope tied from a wooden tripod with a pulley an attached in an A configuration. A bucket was attached to the rope and the guy in the shaft would fill the bucket up with mud that slowed down the flow of the water. They were very kind to me. They told my husband that they could lower me into the shaft to get a better view of the insides. I laughed and told them that I would love to do that but I was afraid of the ground falling in on me. There was no shoring up of wood to make their jobs safer. They had to deal with that uncertainty every day of their lives. They offered us tea while we watched them work. This was a job that I had not seen done in America. I felt privileged to be able to just watch the proceedings.

We were not lucky enough to have one of these qanats near the garden my husband created in a suburb of Kashan. We were living there at the time, and I will get into that in a later chapter. His brother owned a 1-acre plot of really dry land nearby. The closest water source was a small spigot about 300 ft away, which required us to combine 3 long spools of water hose to be able to reach and water the land. I thought that the soil was the worst and nothing would grow on it. My husband proved me wrong. With a lot of water and sun, he grew tomatoes, eggplant, figs, pomegranates, and herbs. I was flabbergasted at the things he was able to grow in that soil. I knew that my husband had a green thumb when it came to house plants we had in America, but I did not realize that he should have become a gardener instead. I learned a lot from his talent for gardens.

I loved to go explore the countryside and get away from the dirty, sandy cities. There were many sprawling dirt roads everywhere that were well worn from all the traffic. The desert flatland was akin to route 66 in America, with long stretches of road, occasional mountains in the distance, and small brush vegetation almost everywhere. Just like one might stop at a diner on route 66, we would come across a little oasis with a stream with a few trees and picnic there.

We weren't the only people doing this, and occasionally we would cross paths, share food, stories, and laughter with other families. The water was always so cold, even in this arid environment. As we explored the desert, we would frequently come across small villages, with less than 100 people.

With me being the curious type, I wanted to see the architecture and culture. We would stop, park, and then walk through village. I took my husband to places in Iran he would have never thought to visit because of my overwhelming curiosity. When people found out that I was a foreigner, they would stop whatever they were doing and spread out a flowery plastic table cloth on the shady part of the ground for us to sit and relax. The women would bring out hot tea, sweets, and whatever food they have ready for eating. I asked my husband if this happens all the time to him when he is traveling. He said no. The villagers are generous and want to show that they have chivalric behavior toward foreigners. Iran had been given a bad name from the revolution and the average Iranian wanted people from other places to know that it was not true. If it was late into the evening, they would even start a fire for us. You must  remember that in an arid climate even though the day is very hot, the night could get cold.

A few weeks later, we stopped to visit a friend from the factory my husband worked at. It was a small walled subdivision just outside of Kashan. We were sitting and having refreshments when of a sudden, I heard a loud roar. We had seen some lightening in the distance mountains early that day but had no idea of the rain that was unleased up there.

We ran to listen to where the noise was coming from. The village that we were in was surrounded by a mud wall about eight feet high. To see anything, we had to come out to the main highway to see what the noise was. On the other side of the road, what once was a very dry old river bed, we saw a huge amount of water and debris going by. Literally, we were standing in a desert area where there had been no water in any direction, and in a matter of seconds, we had a large rushing river.

It felt so strange but yet so familiar. I remembered when my family was driving down the main road in El Paso, it started to rain. We were about to drive under a bridge when my dad noticed that another car had gotten struck in the water under the bridge and could not drive on. They had to almost swim to get away from the flooding water from the rain.

In an area of little rain, when it does rain heavily, flash floods occur. I had forgotten about this problem. And it looked like the people living in this area had forgotten, too. As we traveled alongside the old dried-up river bed, people had made their homes just a few yards away from the small stream that was normally there. This was how they got their water. It must have been a very long time since this kind of flood had visited. People had lowered their guard from a lack of flash floods, and had built houses in that dangerous area.

Hossein's cousin lived in a mountain village near where the flooding occurred. We called her to make sure she was OK right after the flash flood. She said she was fine, and the flood didn't hit their village. Two days later we went to go visit her, and along the way we met many people with stories from the flood. Almost all of them were caught unprepared.

A villager told us about two kids playing outside near the little stream. They were digging in the dirt nearby when all of a sudden they heard a train coming and they didn't know from where. Simultaneously, water gushes and sweeps them off their feet. The water surged so quickly, that it threw one of them onto a roof of a house. The other one was pushed downstream with the rest of the debris. It was a day later when they found the body. Houses that had been there alongside the stream for God knows how many years were suddenly gone.

14

The Evil Eye and Other Traditions

Iran is full of unique traditions. You may find some of these practices in other countries nearby. One of them is the belief in the Evil Eye. I have seen variations of this in Greece and Turkey. This tradition has been passed down through generations from the days of Zoroastrianism. The concept of the evil eye is about being a victim of a curse on someone else's behalf. One did not brag about their good luck or achievements, for fear of someone giving them the evil eye. People would not share certain parts of their lives with others because of the 'cheshm khordan' or being struck by the eye.

In Iran, esfand is used to fight against the evil eye. Esfand is a dried herb made from the seeds and dried fruits of Garden Rue or Peganum harmala. This short evergreen plant is found in the Mediterranean and middle Eastern regions. When the flowers dry, in the middle of the petals are some tiny blackish seeds that are purposed to have magical and medicinal usages. It is believed to heal stomach cramps and expel parasitic worms. Burning Esfand releases its warm herbal aroma to soothe the senses and cast away any negative thoughts. So, then you leave the home for a trip or a special occasion, the women of the home would burn some esfand on a round flat metal tray and bring it to the door that you are leaving from. They would wave the tray around you and bless you with some verses from the Koran.

Something else I noticed is the common practice of lying or telling half-truths. Hossein was especially good at doing this. He would not tell what he was doing to a lot of people just in case they gave him the evil eye. He would even lie how things without blinking an eye. He was good at it. A lot of merchants in this area of the world are very good at convincing you to buy something you really don't need or the quality is not up to par. They have the gift of talking and protecting themselves from the evil eye.

Shirin truly believed in the evil eye. Every time one would leave the house on a short trip, she would get the esfand and burn some over the stove. It would smoke and give a woodsy smell. She would say her prayers for the person and move the smoke around them.

I had a turn with the evil eye, too. I had gotten braces on my teeth late in life. I had them removed right before I left for Iran. My dentist tried his best to get my teeth in good order before I left. I did not have bad teeth. I had a gap in between my two front teeth and wanted to close it. It looks pretty good but I did have to wear a retainer at night which I hated. Otherwise, I did not have any problems. Later, I started to notice that if I opened my jaw too wide, I would get

a nerve-tingling in the side of my mouth. One night while I was taking a shower, I was yawning and opening my mouth real wide and had a surging pain from my left lower jaw. I knew that I had pinched my nerve there. It was all my fault. I truly believed that I did not have a dentist nearby to double-check my mouth after the braces came out and the movement of my teeth was having problems with my nerves.

I came out of the shower still hurting on the side of my face. Then I noticed that I had no muscle movement in the side of my face that had the nerve problem. I could not smile on that side. I could not close my eye either. The other side acted normal. It looked like I had a stroke. My sister-in-law Ava came to look. She was not sure what had happened.

Shirin's reaction was that I had gotten the evil eye and immediately got the esfand out and did the ritual of warding off the evil eye. She believed that everyone outside of the family was sending the evil eye to me because of my blond hair and blue eyes. They were jealous. They were jinxing me and giving me a problem I would be ugly. I respected her opinion but I knew what had happened.

I covered one eye that would not close and went to bed. I thought that in the morning it would be better. No, it was still the same when I woke up. Hossein called for a doctor's appointment and got me there in the afternoon. The doctor told Hossein that I probably had damaged my nerve and to give it about a month to get better. What Hossein did not want to tell me was that the doctor said I had permanently damaged it. It was good that I did not know that part of what the doctor had said. I would have worried too much. As Luck would have it though, after a few weeks I could feel a movement coming back to my face slowly. After about a month, I was in full recover. We went back to the doctor to check me out again and he was very happy that I was doing so well. Of course, Shirin was performing the esfand ceremony every time I went out.

Later on, Shirin gave me a necklace that had an 18k gold filigree hollow ball with some esfand seeds in it. It was on a long gold chain. She wanted me to give it to Angela when she got older. She thought that Angela would need protection because she thought that Angela was a beautiful combination of American and Iranian genes.

Another tradition was to have salt in the home. I knew that salt played a part in old European customs, so much so, that also took root in American culture. I found it delightful that Iranians prized salt so much as well. They made good luck charms for the house with blocks of solid salt. In doing some 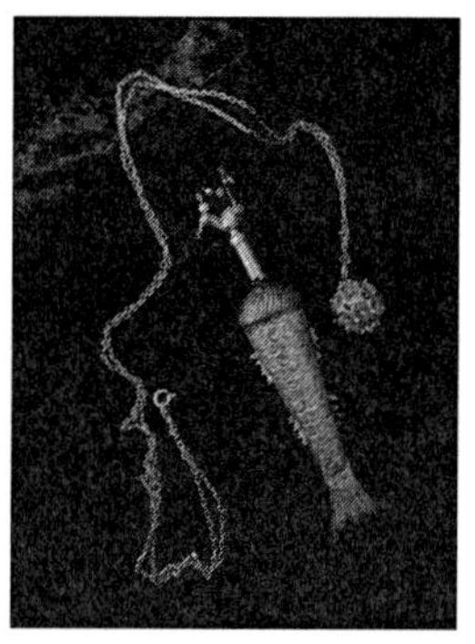 research on the history of salt I read that salt draws bacteria-causing moisture out of foods. It was very useful long ago when we did not have refrigeration for our food. And everyone knows that it adds flavor to savory and sweet dishes of food. It was good manners to offer bread and salt to weary travelers.

One of my husband's cousins was wealthier than the average person in Kashan. Having a business that employed many people, she had to provide special meals or sweets for the staff and family. Just like the turkey dinner and Christmas party here in America, she made Halva (a type of sweet, thick, grainy pudding) every year during the month of Azar. It seemed like she had a ton of it made and had given out to everyone in the neighborhood. During this month, the Islamic prophet Mohammed's grandson was killed. The day of Ashura is very big in Iran as a sorrowful holiday. People will go into the streets chanting Islamic songs and quotes from the Quran (the Islamic version of the Bible).

Halva is also served for funerals or during the month of Ramadan (fasting). It was made with flour, butter, simple syrup, saffron, cardamom, rosewater, and also garnished with slivered almonds. It has a strong sweet taste and helps to increase blood sugar, especially for mourners who may have not eaten for hours or days.

Ramadan is a month of religious fasting as an act of piety. This spiritual month occurs during specific dates on the Islamic calendar. But since Iranian don't use that calendar, the specific dates for Ramadan change each year. This month will occur at different times of the year on the Iranian calendar. Before dawn, everyone gets a healthy breakfast and plenty of liquids to make it until sundown. In Iran, the rules were not too strict as in other Islamic countries. You could not eat out on the streets but you could eat at home. As soon as evening prayers at sunset are called, you may then break your fast. Normally you are offered some sweet dates to start with and then some hot tea. If a woman is on her period or pregnant, she did not have to fast. Young children, the elderly, and the sick did not have to fast. Non-Muslims did not have to fast. It was very prestigious to fast and letting people know that you are fasting made them think more highly of you. Fasting is a form of dedication to God that you will go without food and water and pray to him.

Let me explain the Iranian calendar. It is not the same as ours and not the same year. It is not the same as the Islamic lunar calendar, either. The Iranian calendar is based on the sun and is considered a solar calendar. In 2021, the Iranian year is 1400. It is based on the present-day American calendar year 621 when the Islamic prophet Muhammad and his followers traveled from Mecca to Medina. In the journey, Muhammad is said to have traveled on the back of a winged steed to the farthest mosque to lead other prophets in prayer and then ascends into heaven where he speaks to God. This date is marked as one of the most celebrated dates in the Islamic calendar.

The months:

Farvardin – Mar 21 to April 20	31 days
Ordibehesht – April 21 to May 21	31 days
Khordad – May 22 to June 21	31 days
Tir – June 22 to July 22	31 days
Mordad – July 23 to Aug 22	31 days
Sharivar – Aug 23 to Sept 22	31 days
Mehr – Sept 22 to Oct 22	30 days
Aban – Oct 23 to Nov 21	30 days
Azar – Nov 22 to Dec 21	30 days
Dey – Dec 22 to Jan 22	30 days
Bahman – Jan 21 to Feb 19	30 days
Esfand – Feb 20 to Mar 20	29/30 days

Even though I found that the calendar year was hard to remember, the days of the week were easy. The week started on Saturday. You would work until Thursday afternoon with Friday being the religious day off. So here in Iran, you worked about 5 and one-half days.

Saturday – shanbe (day)
Sunday – yekshanbe (first day)
Monday – doshanbe (second day)
Tuesday – seshanbe (third day)
Wednesday – caharshanbe (fourth day)
Thursday – panjshanbe (fifth day)
Friday – Jom-e (a religious day)

The Iranian new year starts on the first day of Spring which is around the Spring equinox. I always thought that this time of year made more sense than our middle of winter new year. It is the birth of greenery and life. The way they celebrated this time was very different from what we do. The women would create an area with beautifully embroidered cloth. The women would create an area in their house with a beautifully embroidered cloth. On it, along with the Koran, they would put seven items that started with the sound of s. They called it haft-seen (7 s's) and considered it good luck to bless the house and family for the new year. They would put a Koran (meaning wisdom), a mirror and candles for self-reflection and enlightenment, eggs for fertility, wheat (meaning new life), a goldfish swimming in a bowl (representing life's progress), sprouting grass (Sabzeh meaning rebirth) and different types of sweets and fruits. Other items could be Sumac (a seasoning meaning sunrise), Seeb (apple meaning beauty), serekh (vinegar meaning patience, saat (clock meaning time), sekkeh (coin meaning wealth and prosperity), and seer (garlic meaning health and medicine). During this time families would visit other family members and bring small gifts of flowers and sweets. Rose water was sprinkled on a visitor's hands who had taken a long journey to visit them. They will offer hot tea, pumpkin seeds, watermelon seeds, fruit, and some sweets to anyone who comes to visit.

One of the unusual traditions is Chaharshanbe Suri which is celebrated on the eve of the last Wednesday before the Nowruz (the Iranian New Year). At sunset, the families will set out some small bonfires in the neighborhood. They will jump over the flames singing (sorkhi-ye to az man, zardi-ye man az to) which means let your beautiful redness be mine, my paleness (sickly pallor be yours. It is a type of purification practice to begin the new year. It is their hope that doing this will clean themselves of all of the misfortunes and bad spirits of the past year. It is explained that this was from an ancient Zoroastrian rite of Spring and the regeneration of life. They hope the fire will give them enlightenment and happiness. This practice reminds me of the Celtic festival of Bealtaine where jumping the fire keeps the spirits happy and protects the crops and cattle.

Despite the variations in the local traditions, I loved the Iranian people and their feeling of heritage. I had a lack of tradition in my American upbringing. Being a military family and science-oriented, I was introduced to different cultures but never had a strong one in my family. I guess that many people would think that I was lucky to have more freedom in my life. Having a more objective point of view and lack of religious bias, gave me a special insight into how traditions are formed and folklore developed. I can see the mysticism in them and love the beliefs in fairies or Jinns (genie in a bottle).

15

Working Around the House

It was not easy to adapt to life in Iran. I had no family and no friends. My language was developing and still lacked a lot of understanding high leveled conversations. I could talk about shopping and doing work around the house. I can explain what I wanted at the store. I could not talk about philosophy and discuss the laws of the land with most everyone. I had only my husband, his brother, and his wife who could speak English. Even though they had studied English for many years and could speak English fluently, they had trouble talking about high leveled things, too. Of course, with their experience, they were doing much better than me.

My sister-in-law Shirin acted like my adopted mom and showed me a lot about how women in Iran did their house work. I loved her so much for teaching me. The basics were the same, but specifics varied wildly. They cleaned the toilet and other areas of the house much the same way we did here in America. They had bleach and a type of comet cleanser along with a few other cleaning supplies. They did not have the selection of many choices we have here. They only had the basics.

There is one cleaning supply I did not like. It was the broom. We had a vacuum for cleaning the carpets but sand and dirt were always on the steps and back porches. We used a lot of water especially in Tehran to wash the black soot off the tiles. It was a constant battle. If I went barefoot outside in the back of the house on tiles, my feet would be black. The broom that was used was a hand broom very similar to ours but with no longer handle. You would have to bend over to sweep. I saw a lot of older ladies with bent backs and I would venture to guess that this broom helps to cause their backs to be so curved. We finally found a foreign broom for me in one of the markets but it was not common.

Hossein got a job in Kashan at a local carpet company that operated machines to create Persian carpets. As a part of the deal to work there, they provided us rent-free housing. It was on an enclosed dead-end street with a guard at a gatehouse. He wouldn't let anyone other than residents in, and if we had guests he would call us to make sure they could come in. It had been made for foreigner engineers for the factory but they had all left because of the war. We had one of the nice houses that was connected in a row with four others, each with a diving a wall to separate them. It was like a duplex, but with five instead of two, made for the factory upper management. There were about ten houses on the street. A playground was located at the end of the street, with a bomb shelter built underneath it because of the war. Everyone living on this street worked for the factory. We had engineers, business people like Hossein, and religious leaders all living together.

I did love the place. I felt protected by the guard at the gate. I developed some close friends with some of the ladies on the street. All of our kids would have birthday parties together and we had lots of lady tea parties. We could easy walk to each other homes without worrying about traffic. The ladies loved to invite me to their soirees. I normally dressed in blue jeans and a nice blouse while they were dressed to conquer the Paris runways under their chadors.

I listened a lot to my BBC and Voice of America when I got the chance. I remembered one important event occurring in America that I was going to miss. I was very excited when I hear a teacher was scheduled to go up in the shuttle. It was January 28, 1986. I did not actually listen to the take-off on the radio. I was busy doing things around the house. Some of my neighbors came over and told me the about the explosion of the shuttle. All lives were lost. I was very sad to hear this news. My neighbor ladies made sure that I was alright and comforted me.

I had climbed our house's ladder to the top of the flat roof of our house one day to survey the area around us since we were enclosed with a brick wall. I enjoyed seeing the mountains and layout of the area from the roof. In the distance, I noticed a big mud hill and I was curious about its history and purpose. After researching I found that it was called Tepe Sialk. According to records I found in Kashan, archaeologists from France had explored it during the 1950s. It was dated to be around 6000 to 5500 B.C.E. It was completely isolated from anyone.

I told Hossein that Angela and I were going to explore it while he was at work. "Be careful of the little wild things you might encounter," he said. I laughed. We had already seen a snake come into our bathroom through the drain in the middle of the floor and a huge sun spider fall from one of our upper cabinets, land on my foot, and run out of the room. I handled those problems with the gusto of a professional girl scout. My only major concern would be scorpions so we would have to tread very carefully. I took some water and a snack and told one of the neighbor ladies where we were headed just in case of some accident happened. We were explorers in an ancient world and would enjoy ourselves.

Angela and I went through a small gate at the end of the street and traveled through some dry terrain to get to the site. Getting there was a little farther than I thought. It was like driving in Texas. You can see the lights at night in the  distance and think that it is not far, but you would be driving for an hour before you got to those lights. I did not have a cell phone with me in this decade so if we got into trouble, I did not have a way to let someone know. I was going to chance it. Finally, after going to dried-out fields of plants, we got there. It was a big mound of dirt, and much bigger than I thought. It looked like many large buildings made of mud had once been there, but now you could not tell actually what was what. According to my research, it used to be a palace that kings would vacation in to get away from their responsibilities. We climbed up to near the top of the mound and viewed the area. Angela was scrambling all around exploring the site. We could see for miles around. It was breathtaking to see the mountains against the edges of the developing city. It was a very dry area but there were a few trees and green plants running on each side of the stream near our buildings.

I did not find much but there were pieces of pottery everywhere. According to researchers in the 1950s, it was built because of the pristine large water sources nearby. The same water that we had just put our feet in to cool ourselves from the summer heat. The Cheshmed ye Soleiman (Solomon's Spring) has been bringing water from the nearby mountains for thousands of years. All of the sites had been thoroughly excavated and the important finds had been taken. This was a dream come true for me. I loved that I was able to explore something this old. I also wanted to go to Egypt to see the Sphinx and the pyramids. For a while, I had that chance to be that archaeologist making a new discovery. Of course, I was watching for scorpions while we scrambled around the man-made hill. We had been gone for about two hours. I thought that we better return before we had an accident.

Back in the real world, I still loved this area even though I did not have the luxuries of home in America. We were living very modestly compared to others which was good. No one could point to us, be jealous and give us the evil eye (smile). We could afford very little furniture. We had about four chairs and one big bed from Tehran that was actually two single mattresses put together into one king-size bed frame. The carpet factory gave us three large carpets to put in the main rooms and of course, I had my kitchen supplies and clothes.

We had very little else for our three bedrooms, two baths (including a foreign-style toilet like home in America), a large foyer, a dining room, and a living room.

We closed off the living and dining rooms because we had nothing to put in there. We used only two of the bedrooms and left the third room as a storage place for our luggage and other things. We used the foyer as our main living place. It had a built-in bookcase to put the books that I had brought from home so it was my favorite room. We had one of the carpets in it with the four chairs. I hung pictures up on the walls to make it feel homely.

I was very lucky that I took home economics in middle school. This is where I learned to sew clothes. My mother was never very interested in teaching but I had an interest in it and my teacher assisted me in learning some valuable skills that I use up to this day. In Iran, they have plenty of clothes you can buy but they can be very cheap or very expensive. During my stay in Iran, I may have brought a couple of t-shirts and that is all over four years. If I needed something, I would make it myself. This is what happened to Angela and her clothes. I used my second bedroom as my place for sewing. I bought some patterns and a sewing machine from America with me and began to sew. I even had one of Hossein's cousins wanting me to make some clothes for her daughter. It kept me busy. I made bed covers, pillow cases, and curtains for the home.

16

The First Trip to Southern Iran

We finally decided to go on a
road trip to the south of Iran
to show me some of the most
notable places that Iran is
famous for. We had a small
Renault car that carried my
husband, me, my brother-in-
law, his wife, and two small girls. Angela was about one-
year-old and her cousin was about three years old.

We packed very light since we had very little space in
the car. We also packed a small cooler with food. This is not
like America. You cannot find fast food restaurants along
the way here. There were a few stalls and small restaurants
that sold kebab sandwiches. So, we always had water and
food with us if we became hungry.

The first stop on our trip was the town of Natanz. It is
about forty-five miles south of Kashan. I will never forget
this place. It was the only time that we got permission to
climb up a minaret. It was made of brick and the staircase
was made of stone and very narrow. It was an adventure to
climb. I carried Angela and Hossein brought Nahid with us.
Ava took a picture of us at the top. We sat on the parapet

very carefully because the edge of the stone bricks was not very high to secure us. We held tightly to the kids but what a view.

It was the first time that I had looked down upon an old village of mud brick walls and houses. It was breathtaking in its own way. You could see the Karkas mountains a short distance away with a small forest of trees dotting the landscape. It had a dry look to it even though there were trees. It is known for the pear fruit grown here. It was not what we would call lush but still, it was beautiful to me.

We got back on the road. We did not have highways in a lot of the areas going south from Kashan. Some of the roads were all dirt. It could get a little bumpy along the way. It was an adventure. I felt like we were going back in time. We did not know what to expect around the next corner.

I saw hillside caves that had been made into rustic houses. It reminded me of the cave houses in Cappadocia, Turkey but not as pointed. We saw little vegetable stalls along the road selling veggies and fruit. We picked up some Iranian cantaloupe that was yellow and shaped like a football. It was delicious. We drove late into the night until we reached a motel of some sort. It had a few large rooms that families could stay in together. We all got our own beds but we kept our important thing with us in our beds. There were no showers but there were very smelly toilets outside. Needless to say, we did not stay long after we woke up.

Back on the road, we were driving on better roads and it was flatter. Kashan was only about 135 miles away from Isfahan but it took us longer with the not-so-good roads. I had read about Isfahan. It was an old and famous city dating all the way back to the Silk Road time. Its nickname is 'Eshfahan nesf-e-jahan ast' (Isfahan is half of the world). Human habitation in this region has been traced back to the Paleolithic period (roughly 2.5 million years to 10,000 B.C.) It was known for its many bridges over the Zayandeh River. It is the biggest river in the central part of Iran and is about 250 miles long.

One thing that I noticed about the central area of Iran is that you have to plant a tree and take care of it. It will not grow on its own. The weather is too dry and hard to grow a lot unless you help it along the way. Along the main roads in the city, you can see where people had planted trees in front of their stores and houses. Every main road had 2 flowing sources of water. These streams flowed between the sidewalk and where you parked. Think of the curb in America and how water normally flows into gutters. Except these were not waste water and were instead fresh water. Instead of parking next to the curb, you parked next to the stream and it was very easy to accidently put your wheel in it. This was in Isfahan, as well as most other large cities.

We checked into a regular hotel this time. It looked like a couple of motel rooms with very basic things. Nothing to get excited about but at least we did not have to share with anyone. This location was not far from the famous bridges of Isfahan. The names of these bridges over the Zayanderud river are the Shahrestan, Khaju, Choobi, Si-o-ee Pol, and

Marnan Bridges. I did not get to see all of the bridges, but the ones I saw were very unique.

The oldest of the bridges is the Shahrestan Bridge built during the Sasanian Empire between the third to seventh centuries C.E. The Khaju Bridge was my favorite one because you walk in and around it and get your feet wet. Late into the evening, families would gather in these areas next to the river and catch the evening light. They would have a picnic and the kids would play on the steps next to the bottom level of the bridge. It was very calming.

Even though the bridges were famous, it was the main square in Isfahan which is what gets people to visit this grand city. The name has changed many times in line with the current ruling class. Most people called it the Naqsh-e Jahan Square (image of the world), but it is also known as Shah or Imam Square. It was and is stunning.

It was constructed between 1598 and 1629 and is one of UNESCO's World Heritage sites. The buildings that surround the main square were built in the Safavid er of Iran. You have the Shah Mosque (the current name is Imam Mosque) on the southside. On the west side is the Ali Qapu Palace. The eastern side has the Sheikh Lotf Allah Mosque and on the northern side, Qeysarie Gate opens into the Isfahan Grand Bazaar.

This square was part of the Silk Road. Goods from all of the civilized countries flowed through this city to get to the Middle Kingdom (China). Persians were famously gifted merchants who knew how to make the best profits from the goods that passed through this area. This Royal Square was admired by Europeans who visited Isfahan

during Shad Abbas' reign. One visiter from long ago (Pietro Della Valle) conceded that it outshone the Piazza Navona in his native Rome. I would have to agree.

I could sit and look at these buildings for days. They are so beautiful in their own unique way. What I remember about the Ali Qupu Palace are the bottle-shaped holes in the Music Hall. There were enchanting long-necked flasks and perfume jar niches in the walls and ceiling. These deep circular niches have aesthetic and acoustic value to the room. The palace was six floors high and has a difficult spiral staircase that reminds me of the minaret in Natanz. Monarchs from long ago would entertain visitors and foreign ambassadors. From the upper galleries, the rulers could watch army maneuvers and horse-racing in the square. Currently, people have picnics and camp overnight in the square.

The two mosques in the square are very different from each other. The one across from the palace is so beautiful and delicate. It was made to be used more for the ladies of Shah Abbas' harem. There was a tunnel from the palace to the mosque where the women of the harem could go unseen to pray. The walls and ceilings are deckled out in exquisite mosaics. I sat in a corner of one of the rooms to take in the beauty of the room. I could imagine myself back two hundred years dressed in brocade silks and eating dates for a snack. The other mosque is the king's (Shah's) mosque. It is huge and can hold thousands of people in prayer. Still beautiful and awe-inspiring, I was overwhelmed by the size and details of the large vaulted rooms.

The next day we bundled up our things and traveled to Shiraz. It is about three hundred miles south of Isfahan. It took us all day to get there. We went through mountain passes into valleys along the way. It was a stunning drive. The mountains were not as high as the Rocky Mountains but they were very neat to see. We saw fire temples on some of the tops of the mountains and caves on the sides of the mountains which were for ancient homes. I was so excited to get out of the big cities and see the countryside.

We settled into our hotel for the evening and picked up some kabab with flat bread and veggies. The beds were hard and but I was young and could handle it. In Shiraz, there were several famous palaces and mosques and we spent a day exploring them. Shiraz is also famous for flowers, literature, and two of Iran's notable poets, Hafez and Saadi. We visited the shrine of Saadi, in which my sister-in-law translated some of the poems etched in the marble tomb. He

was not only a poet but philosopher and absolute master of the Farsi language. One of his famous poems is written at the entrance of the United Nations building in New Yor. It begins "All human beings are members of the frame, since all, at first, from the same essence came. When time afflicts a limb with pain, the other limbs cannot remain, If thou feel not for other's misery a human being is no name for thee."

The big international draw to Shiraz was just about 60 miles outside of the city. It was the great palace of Darius I in 518 B.C.E. Its name is Persepolis and is also a UNESCO World Heritage site. It was the capital of the Achaemenid Empire. The buildings were sitting on an immense terrance and successive kings erected a series of architecturally stunning palatial buildings. A couple of the buildings were the massive Apadana palace and the Throne Hall (hundred Column Hall). Alexander the Great burned this palace down in 330 B.C. Even with the burning, I could tell that it must have been a beautiful place. It had been an immense set of buildings. We roamed around for hours.

Not far from this site were four tombs carved into the rockface of a mountain. There are ancient necropolis houses called Naqsh-e Rustam. I felt like I was in Egypt. It was so large. They were like giant crosses carved into the mountain and so the site is locally known as the 'Persian Crosses.' It is thought to be the burial place of Persian kings; Darius I the great, Xerxes 1, Artaxerxes, and Darius 11. There was also a Zoroastrian fire temple near the tombs we were able to see up close. It reminded me of the temple we tried to climb up to on the way to Kashan. I did not realize that we would be able to see one so close.

Down the road about an hour away, were the ruins of Pasargadae, the capital of the Achaemenid Empire under Cyrus the Great (559–530 B.C.E). Again this area is another UNESCO World Heritage Site. Down the road about another mile and a half is the mausoleum of Cyrus which looks like a stone house set on some pyramid steps. There was a column in the Pasargadae complex that had a stork's nest on the top.

I could go on and on about these ancient buildings but you see to pictures from the internet. It is not easy for  Americans to travel to Iran right now. I can only say that I will always remember walking through them and being so awe-struck.

17

Northern Iran and the Fine Crafts

Although we did most of our trips around Iran toward the southern part of the country, we did have a very short trip to the city of Rasht and the Caspian Sea. Again we loaded up the small Renault with four adults, two kids, bags, and food to eat along the way. Fast food places were not everywhere and forget about drive-through places. There was no such thing at that time. Before we started, I explored the map of how we were to travel. There was this road we were going on named the Chaloos Highway (Route 59). It is about 100 miles of twists, turns, tunnels, and spectacular landscape through the Alborz Mountains. It was almost scary with all of the hairpin turns coming off the mountainous side and going into the luxuriant valley full of vegetation. The south of Iran is very dry in climate, but here is where it is lush and green. I was immersed and surprised at how beautiful this road was. It made the

crammed car tolerable. We drove from Tehran to the town of Chalus right net to the Caspian Sea.

Hossein had explained to me that during the days of the Shah being in power, women went to the shoreline of the sea in bikinis. Of course, under the new rulership, it is not the same. He explained that now they have to section off a part of the beach with long big black tarps so the women could swim without men looking. I thought this was fine. I decided instead of a swimsuit, to go into the water with my blue jeans and a shirt on. Dressing modestly in a country like this would be a good decision.

We found the area designated for women. My sister-in-law and I took our girls with us to the sheltered women-only side of the tarps. We put all of our things down. There were quite a few other women nearby. I took off my chador and was about to take my scarf off when a woman came up yelling at me. I was very confused. My body was still covered with all of my other clothes. I just wanted to get the sun on my face. There were no men that I could see in the area. I had been told that women could see each other but no men. She told my sister-in-law that we must keep our scarves and chador on. Now I got angry. I had studied to the best of my ability the rules and what was allowed according to Islamic law. This lady did not even know her own religious laws.

I argued that the tarps were there to separate us from the men. I was not putting on a swimming suit. Why were we not allowed the freedom of no scarves? Where in the Quran says that women could not see each other? She insisted that we had to remain covered. I turned and said in Farsi that she was crazy and to the devil with this separation. I left the women's side, with chador still off (still in full clothing with a scarf covering my head). I was going back to swim in the Caspian Sea and be with my husband. We collected our

things and left to join my husband. We got back to them, explained what had happened, laughed at the rules, found our own secluded spot on the beach, and then went swimming in the sea. No one bothered me for taking my veil off with my husband around.

The Caspian Sea was a place that I had wanted to travel to. It is not impressive but I felt like I was very close to Russia. I was seeing the world, bit by bit. The only thing that I could say about the Caspian Sea is that it is known for its Beluga Sturgeon fish which produces some of the most famous caviar and most expensive in the world. Let's get one thing straight. I do not like caviar, but I love to study different species of animals around the world. The Beluga Sturgeon is a large prehistoric fish that can reach 15 feet long. Iranian caviar is something I have always heard about and I wanted to at least say I had been there. The Caspian Sea had a muddy look to it. It looked very gloomy and good for fishing only.

Iran is known for other products and crafts, too. Of course, the delicate flavor of red saffron, rose water, dried limes, and sumac are top-notch quality items. Walking around the bazaars and markets you can smell the richness of the spices. A quick note about opium. The poppy flower is grown in different regions of this country and is considered illegal. I did understand that there were quite a few older people addicted to it. I got to meet one of these guys. He showed me how he applied the opium and lit up his type of pipe. I guess if you need something bad enough, you will find a way to get it no matter where you are.

Another craft that the Iranians prized is the art of Inlay Khatan. They cut them into long triangular sticks, and then build a pattern and glue it together. Then they cut the glued wooden pattern into various shapes and sizes depending on the object they are creating, but usually thing discs for tiles or flat surfaces. Then they add very finely cut brass and gold trim to whatever object they are making. This ingenious method of cutting wood requires great precision and steady hands to do this. It dates back as far as the fifteenth century in Iran. A lot of Reza Shah's furniture was made this way.

Of course, everyone has heard about Persian rugs. Even little kids know about the flying Persian carpet from the story of Aladdin. You could have machine-made rugs, but anyone who was anyone had handmade carpets in their homes in Iran. Almost all of the Iranian carpets are made with lots of flowers, medallions, and the paisley design of Persian origin. Along with tapestries that were heavy embroidered with gold and silver, they were designed with rich symbolism. Most carpets would be made of wool, but being on the silk road, the finer carpets were double-knotted with silk.

Metalwork is also a favorite craft of Iranian. The hammering of tin or copper can be heard throughout the bazaar. Table tops and ornate samovars for making traditional tea are everywhere in the bazaar to purchase. Gold is also very prized. Women used to wear their wealth with gold bracelets, rings, and necklaces. It was common that when there was a special occasion like a marriage, you give gold. Here in America, we buy 10 to 14k gold. There, they buy 18 to 24k gold. The practice is not as common nowadays, though. When Angela was born, I received a lot of little gold bracelets for her.

Persian architecture is beyond understanding. The buildings that I have walked into had dazzling geometric symmetries, awe-inspiring niches, and domed ceilings. The architects had put their passion and ingenuity to create undeniable aesthetic and decadent designs for the many buildings.

Along with the crafts of Iran, Persian music and poetry were exported all around the world. Poets like Omar Khayyam, Ferdosi, Saadi, and Hafez are known outside the Persian realm for their pose and love of gardens and romance. Ferdosi was inspired by older epic works like Beowulf and created a Persian national epic named the Shahnameh. It is one of the longest epic poems created by a single poet. If you ever get any copy of the books of poems and pose, it will be full of exquisite paintings of women and wine. And by the way, words are written from right to left and the back of the book is actually the front. Even though I never got to read the words very well, I tried to learn to write the alphabet.

With all of this influence in poetry from the past, I started to realize that Hossein had a musical way of talking almost like poetry. I guess that it was one way he had interested me and I loved his voice. I wish now that I had recorded the way he would say things. It was very alluring and I could listen to him tell a story for hours. The Persian language is very similar to Arabic. It has guttural sounds in many of its words but a musical way of saying these words is more pleasant to the ears. I can relate the sounds of English and French in comparison to the different sounds in Arabic and Farsi. I think that the french people can say their words in a more seductive way than the English people. Of course, there are always exceptions to this thought.

Here are some thoughts on the religions of Iran. Most people think of Islam as the only religion. The Iranians were mostly of the Shite sect of Islam while the majority of Islamic people around the world are of the Sunni sect of Islam. It does play a lot in politics today. The division occurred after their prophet Muhammad died. His successor was disputed. One section believed that Ali (his son-in-law) should be the next caliph and another section wanted Abu Bakr to be caliph. This led to a major split in Islam and the Iranians have always been sat apart from the Arabic culture due to this split, history of culture, and language. Although the Persian language sounds similar, they are not the same. Iranians consider it an insult to be classified or grouped with Arabic countries.

The oldest monotheism religion in the world is considered to be Zoroastrianism which originated in ancient Persia. The prophet Zoroaster dated back to somewhere between 1500 and 1200 B.C.E. He had a divine vision and began teaching followers to worship a single god called Ahura Mazda. Fire plays an important part in this religion. Fire represents God's light or wisdom. Instead of ritual worship, they focus on the central ethics of 'good thoughts and good deeds.' To this day, there are followers of this religion around the world. In some of the places I traveled to in Iran, I got to see the evidence and motifs of this religion all around the historic sites. The cypress trees were venerated as a tree of everlasting life and weaved into carpets and placed in many Persian gardens.

According to the Iranian government, they recognize only Islam, Christianity, Judaism, and Zoroastrianism as official religions. If you are in any other religion, you do not have equal rights in Iran. For example, we had some neighbors in Tehran that spoke English. I was excited to be able to speak to others outside the family. They invited Hossein and me over one afternoon for some tea. I very much enjoyed visiting them. They were of the Baha'i faith. Their religion was all about harmony and unity in the world. When we got home, my sister-in-law made me wash my hands thoroughly. She considered the neighbors unclean. My brother-in-law came home and forbade us to go visit again. My husband and I were shocked at this behavior. I was not quite understanding what was bad about their faith. Luckily, we were living in Kashan now so we could not go to the neighbors for another visit at that time. It caused a rift between the two brothers, and Hossein did not speak to his brother for almost six months. I found out much later that properties from Baha'i families had been confiscated, cemeteries destroyed and universities refused to admit Baha'i students. My sister-in-law at school was even directed to identify who was Baha'i Again, I never understood why the persecution.

18

The War

I did come to Iran during the Iran-Iraq war. All of my family asked me if I was crazy to go there at this juncture in time. That is why Hossein went first to Iran. He had to see his mother because of her stroke and he wanted to see how the war was affecting Tehran before I considered going there to meet the family.

The only thing noteworthy difference was the rationing of food, but we could handle that with little problem. There were no bombing raids at this time in Tehran but people were being cautious. It looked like the war had subsided for a while and Hossein was gung-ho about me coming to Iran. He had family members who were doctors and I would get the best care when I delivered my baby. He had no worries, so I joined him.

I would say at the time that I came; there was no trace of war in Tehran. The war was at the border between the two countries about 500 miles west and 400 miles south of us. During wartime, almost any country needs to ration certain things, and Iran was no different. America had an embargo on Iran and was supporting Iraq with military aid which was not comforting to me. America sided with Iraq because the Iranians had overthrown the Shah that they had supported.

We would watch the Iranian news on T.V. and hear about the soldiers that had died for protecting the country. Iraq was the invader. To say it simply, Saddam Hossein, the leader of Iraq wanted the Iranian oil fields. Iran was not going to be bullied. With the overthrow of the Shah of Iran, Iraq thought that Iran would be weak and vulnerable. It was a good time to strike while the Americans would not support Iran because of the Hostage Crisis of 1979. Of course, there were more details to this war than what I have mentioned but I am not an expert on these things. This is was I heard from the people on the streets of Iran and what they believed.

On September 22, 1980, Iraq attacks Khuzestan Province in the southwest part of Iran. Khuzestan was and is the major oil-producing region of Iran. It holds 80% of Iran's onshore oil reserves and 57% of Iran's total oil reserves. Iran was not going to lose this area without a fight. Iran blamed the U.S. for the invasion and called it an American plot to encourage another Muslim country to attack them.

During the summer, the war started to rev up again. My sisters-in-law had placed tape shaped like Xs on all the windows just in case of a bomb went off somewhere nearby. If the window broke, the tape would help the glass pieces from flying too far. We started to have bombing raids in the late evenings. We had to put heavy black curtains on the windows to prevent any light from escaping so people wouldn't know we were home. Iran had had effectively announced martial law, and had imposed a lockdown on visible lights during the night. The street lights were turned off, too.

Sirens would start sounding off at night. We would grab everyone and take cover under the stairwell between our two apartments. It was a very narrow hallway and the door to the outside was nearby if we had to get out of the building. We had a foam mattress that we would put on one side of ourselves in case of any glass hit us.

We could feel an occasional bomb drop somewhere a few miles from us. At this point in time, I slept with Angela in my arms. If she was going to die, I would be right beside her. This was the best I could do to protect ourselves in this situation. We could not get a flight out of Iran at this point, because they were attacking the airport.

I was told that if we could hear the bombings, we were safe. But if we could hear whistling, that was a bad sign. It meant that we were in the direct path of the bomb. I do not have enough experience to say if that was true or not. I only felt bombs maybe a half dozen times dropping. I think that Iraq was trying to scare Iranians to show they could fly all the way to the capital if needed. They flew up high in the sky as the anti-craft carrier missiles could not shoot them down very easily.

When we were living in Kashan, we were farther away from the war. This was a smaller city with no military importance. We felt quite safe there for almost 2 years, until the war found us.

I was talking on the phone with my husband's cousin. We were discussing some outfits that she would like me to make for her teenage daughter. All of a sudden, we heard overhead some deafening sounds. We were not sure what it was but our ears were hurting. I hung up the phone and grabbed my daughter and a friend she had over to play with. I got us into an archway of our home as fast as I could. I could feel the earth moving like an earthquake but I knew better. The sounds finally left in what felt like minutes but were really just about 30 seconds. I look out of my door and could see a dust fume rising not far from our street in the desert. I knew that it was a number of jets flying real low that attacked our town.

Luckily, we did not live in the main part of town. We lived on the outskirts. The dust plume that we saw so close to us, ended up not being a bomb, but just a spent fuel tank they dropped to speed up their escape. We were not sure what exactly had happened. I did not know what part of the town was hit. I knew that my husband was at work in the Kashan Carpet factory closer to town. The group of ladies that lived near me was all gathered in the street also worried about their husbands.

Finally, our husbands were returning home to us. They were happy to see that we were safe, and vice versa. It took a while before we found out what had happened. According to eye witnesses, five Iraqi jets flew low to avoid radar detection. This explained why there was such an unusual loud noise. It looks like they used cluster missiles or bombs coming into town. They hit a mosque near the bazaar and several homes.

I am not sure how many people were injured from this attack, but there were some people in a bread line that got killed. The biggest story was about a dentist in his office. When the attack happened, he grabbed the kids in his office and put them under his desk. They survived but he did not.

It was so sad. We drove around the town to see what effect the bombing did to the town. I will never forget it. Saddam Hossein had made his point that no part of Iran was safe until he got what he wanted.

Instead of being afraid, it just made more young men volunteer to beat the tyrant back. It reignited the passion and anger of Iranians to put an end to this bloodshed. It was their land and they were going to fight for it. It was almost a decade long conflict with tons of back forth, and even for someone like me who lived through it, I would be lying if I said I knew all the details. But in broad strokes, Iraq invaded Iran and Iran retaliated and wouldn't accept Iraq's ceasefire for many years. One of the most egregious acts of was when Iraq started using chemical weapons against Iranian troops along with some of its own dissenters. They released chemicals in March 1988, killing as many as 5,000 families in the Kurdish village of Halabja.

America made a mistake in backing President Saddam Hussein of Iraq. They also shot down Iran Air Flight 655, a passenger airbus type plane on July 3, 1988. It was scheduled to fly from Tehran to Dubai via Bandar Abbas. All 290 people on board were killed. The USS Vincennes had incorrectly identified the Airbus as an attacking F-14 Tomcat. President Ronald Reagan issued a written diplomatic note to the Iranian government expressing deep regret for the mistaken identity. The U.S. still insisted the Vincennes was acting in self-dense in international waters. In 1996, the U.S. did finally agree to pay $61.8 million dollars to the families of the Iranian victims.

Only because of Iran's deteriorating economy, did Iran accept a United Nations-mediated cease-fire in August of

1988. The Iranian leader Ayatollah Khomeini dies on June 4, 1989. The withdrawal of troops did not take place until the signing of a formal peace agreement on August 16, 1990.

The Iran–Iraq war did not change the border. Neither country got any reparations, but about 500,00 soldiers and about 100,000 civilians died in the fighting. To me, Saddam Hossein of Iraq was someone America should have never supported. Me and Iran's view of him was even more justified when he annexed Kuwait for its oil fields in the same month they signed the peace agreement with Iran. I was not a fan of Saddam Hussein. On December 13, 2003, American Operation Red Dawn conducted a raid on the town of ad-Dawr in Iraq which led to the capture and arrest of former Iraqi president Saddam Hussein.

19
Back in America

It had been about three and a half years since I had been back home. I was getting homesick. My daughter had turned three and none of my family had been able to see her except in pictures. I started to pester my husband about this problem. Before we moved to Iran, he had promised me that I would be able to visit my family every other year. I knew that we did not have a lot of money, but I needed him to figure out how to get me and Angela there for a spell.

He took me to one of the government's offices in Tehran that could give us a discounted airplane ticket. He talked to them but they did not want to help. So, Hossein told me to stay and act sad and upset. He would come back after a while. I sat and literally was crying to myself thinking about how I was home sick. One of the government officials brought me into a room and a religious leader in a black turban working with the officials asked me something. I could not explain or understand the question he was asking me. He started to demonstrate taking off a ring from his finger. I finally understood he was asking me if I wanted a divorce. I shook my head and said no. I just did not know how to say that I was homesick. Hossein came back after about 30 minutes. He talked with them for a few more moments. They still would not do anything for us. Hossein explained to me that they had asked me if I wanted a divorce. "Sorry," I said. I was so upset and could not explain to them why I was crying.

I did not want to do something like that again. I feel so alone in that room. I told Hossein that I wanted to be home for Christmas and show Angela, my family. I do not know how he was able to get tickets, but he had reservations on Iranair for us two to leave out in October. Our plans were to stay about three to four months and then return. Our round-trip tickets were good for one year.

I went to the Swiss Embassy American Interest Section to ask how the passport situation should be handled. We needed to fly out using our Iranian passports, and then they were going to have our American passports sent ahead and be awaiting us in Geneva, Switzerland. We would fly into Zürich, take a connecting flight to Geneva and they would provide us our American passports for the rest of the trip. The Iranian government at this time was not letting any Americans with American passports in and out of the country. The Swiss Embassy recommended that we send out our passports through their couriers so the Iranian government did not confiscate our American passports at the airport when they searched us. I had to travel on an Iranian passport. Hossein had to get a document signed and stamped that he was letting us out of the country on our own since women and children could not travel without their husband's permission.

I was so excited to go. Angela at this point in her little life understood English but basically spoke Farsi. This was going to get her some experience listening to other

Americans and pick up the language better. Hossein saw us off. We had no problems on our trip. As soon as I got off the plane in Zurich, and changed to Swiss Air, I took off my covering. Angela looked at me. 'Mother, cover up before someone sees you.' I laughed. "Love, in this part of the world, women do not have to cover up." She was confused but accepted it.

I have blue eyes. Everyone in Iran that I had met had brown eyes. I was amazed. I was seeing blonde hair and blue-eyed people everywhere. It was as if this was so strange to me. I had been in a vacuum. I had not seen the latest fashion or hairstyles. National news on the monitors not pertaining to the Iranian war was weird. I was so happy to hear about other countries on the T.Vs in the terminal. I was happy to be going home for a while.

Back in America, I stayed with my dad. My daughter and I stayed in the basement of my dad's home in the northern part of Atlanta. I decided to get a Christmas job at a kid's clothing and toy store. My family would take care of Angela while I was working. I wanted to buy somethings to take back with us. Luckily, my dad had a moped that I was able to ride on. At this job, I was able to purchase a few special dolls for Angela and her cousin. Angela's first nice doll was named 'Patty' and her cousin named her doll 'Aazeetaa' when we eventually got back to Iran. I purchased quite a few beautiful dresses for them, and some updated clothes for me. I had not purchased any new clothes in Iran. We simply did not have the extra money. So, this was a real treat for me.

Christmas came and I started to plan our return trip back to Iran. Hossein called me just after Christmas and say,

"Wait, I am coming. We will stay in America for a year or two, and save some money to take back." Over there you could live on $200 easily a month. If we had a couple of thousand dollars to take with us that would really get us ahead.

He also told me about a guy who came to him and talked about a temporary marriage that he could have when I was gone. I was so proud of him. He told that guy that he was very much in love with my wife and would not consider it. I had to do some research on this Sigheh or nikah mut'ah in Arabic. It allows men to marry a woman for a pre-determined period of time and have intimate relations with her. To me, it sounded like a loophole for prostitution. According to Iranian Civil Law article 1075, men aged 15 or older and women aged 13 and older can enter into such a relationship. A sigh can last for one hour, a few days a few months, or longer. Sounds like old fashion prostitution to me. How could the man be guaranteed that a woman was not being forced to do this sigheh by others making money off of her?

Hossein came to Atlanta in January and went back to work at his old work working for a carpet factory in Carterville, Georgia. I took a job as an assistant at a clothing store. After about three months, he had to get a physical to renew his green card to continue working since he was not an American citizen. We put my daughter in a pre-k class so she has some instruction in English from a regular teacher.

While she was at school, we went to the doctors for the checkup. The doctor noticed something on his lungs and they wanted to refer him to a specialist. His insurance from his work had just kicked in which was good timing. He had an appointment about three weeks later. At this point in life, Hossein and I were pretty healthy. I would jog around the parks and Hossein focused on weight lifting. One day he decided to jog with me. After a short distance, he started limping and was in very deep pain. We called the specialist and accelerated our appointment to as soon as possible.

At the doctors, they x-rayed his hip and leg and said it was not good. Something was eating at his bone and the hip was deteriorating. He could not walk at this point. They put him in an ambulance and sent him to Emory University Hospital. There, they did all sorts of tests, and by the end of the day several doctors came out to talk to me. They explained that Hossein had advance lung cancer and it had already spread to the bones. "What?" I said. I could not understand. This was a shocker to me. He was not and never was a smoker. He was healthy up to this point. What happened? They shrugged their shoulders and could not explain. This was the late 1980s. Cancer was still being explored and there were a lot of unanswered questions for everyone.

Maybe he had worked around asbestos. Maybe he had injured his lungs in a sporting event. So many questions and we could only guess the answers. The doctors explain that he would go through chemotherapy but they did not have high hopes. He was very advanced in the stages of cancer. I asked the main cancer doctor a point-blank question. How long does he have to live? The doctor replied, "five to six months." I soaked this answer into my soul. Hossein did not want to hear any of this. He believed that he would beat it. The doctors told us that they would try everything to beat cancer. The first step was to get a hip replacement to replace the bone that had been eaten by this disease. He was in the hospital for about a week. The doctors told him that the next step is having some very strong chemo treatments and radiation afterward.

The chemo began. They predicted that he would lose his hair. He would be very weak. They had put him on the strongest chemo possible at that time to try. He was a guinea pig. He was young and strong and they watched how his body reacted. All I could say was that he was very resilient, and took the chemo like a champ. He lost just a little bit of his hair, and he became very fragile. He wanted to sleep but his body ached all over. I had to be careful when I touched him.

He called his family in Iran and explained the situation. He was going to fight this and it was good that he was in America with the more advanced technology on cancer. They were so upset and rightfully so. How could such a young healthy person have this problem? How did he get it? They just like me had so many questions and no answers.

I called Mohammed when Hossein was out on a grocery run. I explained what the doctors had said about five to six months. I could hear Mohammed crying on the phone. I told him as soon as Hossein had finished all of his chemo and radiation treatments, we would come home.

After the last treatment, the doctors x-rayed him again and did more tests. The results came back very bad. Not only had the cancer gotten worse, but it had also spread to create tumors on his head. Thank God that I had curled Hossein's hair to make an afro style. It covered the bumps on his head. We have scheduled radiation treatments in

Rome, Georgia twice a week after that as a last resort. Again, the results came back with no improvement. It had only gotten worse.

Finally, the doctors had no more treatments for him. I told them not to say anything to him. He had faith in being healed and nothing was going to stop it. I wanted him to keep his confidence in God that he was going to get better. Hope was all he had now. I made plans. My airplane ticket for Angela and I would expire soon. I had to get him home. I called the airlines and made the reservations for the very last day we could stay in America. The day that we were supposed to arrival in Tehran was the day after our tickets expired. The airlines say along as you had started your trip, the tickets are good. I was still worried.

I waited about five days before we were about to leave. I sat Hossein down. I explained that the doctors had no more treatments for him. All we could do now is to go home back to his family and pray. We needed his family's support to help him through this devastating time.

<h1 style="text-align:center">20</h1>

<h1 style="text-align:center">Back in Iran</h1>

We were all packed up and ready to go. My family advised me not to go back to Iran. Hossein would better off in America given his situation. They were afraid that once Hossein died, I would have difficulties leaving Iran with my daughter. I said that Hossein needed his family. They would need closure with him. I would do what I had to do. I loved him very much. Hossein understood the fears my family had. He wrote a letter that I was to give my brother-in-law after he died telling Mohammed to make sure Angela and I were able to go back to America.

Hossein felt like this was goodbye to America. I checked with the immigration services that we were leaving the U.S. and to stop the green card renewal process. They said, "Are you sure? He may win against this battle." I was very sad. It was hard to explain what the doctors had said. I told them to thank you for double-checking but I had little hope from what the doctors had said.

We checked into the Atlanta airport. Hossein was starting to have breathing problems. It was not getting better. I had gotten all of the morphine and any other medication he might have needed for the trip. I did not want to rely on what was in Iran at this point. We had a layover

151

of 9 hours in Frankfurt, Germany. Hossein was extremely tired. We were lucky to get into a special waiting room for Lufthansa customers. He laid down on a bench while Angela was playing on the floor with some other passengers' kids. His breathing was getting worse.

I check us into our final leg of the journey with IranAir who then told us that our tickets were expired. I explained that the other airline told us that our tickets were still good along as we were still on our trip. I also explained the situation of my husband. I said them that he wanted to be with his family. He was dying of cancer. They looked at him lying down and called someone about our situation. Thank God, he was looking out for us again. They let us continue on our quest to get him home.

I had to put on my chador again. I had to get my husband, my child, and all my carry-on luggage on the plane by myself. After stowing everything away, and buckling up my husband and child, I plopped down into my seat. After eighteen hours of travel, I crashed into some sleep. I woke up only after Angela was telling me it was time for some food. It was nice to get some Iranian food after being away from it for almost a year.

Hossein had done his best to let me get some sleep. His breathing was getting worse by the hour. I knew that it would not be long before he would have to be on oxygen. I just had to get him home. I could not see anything or do anything else until I had accomplished this task. His family had to see him before something happened.

He was able to eat a little from what encouragement I could give him. "You have to eat," I said. "You will see your family soon and you want to have some energy to talk and be with them." He would take a bite, breathe a little, and then another bite. It took a long time for him to finish as best as he could. The stewardess wanted to take his tray and I had to explain that he was sick and having trouble eating. She was kind enough to leave us alone until the flight was about to land. We had made it.

The next step was getting us off the plane. This airport did not have an airplane drive-up to a concourse of any kind. We had to get down the stairs, get on a mini-bus, and then to the terminal. So, I collected all of our things, including my daughter, and turned to Hossein. He could not breath very well. I told him if he could muster the energy to get up, one of the attendants would help us get to the bus. We were the last ones off of the plane. The airport officials were very kind to us. We finally got Hossein out into the waiting room where Mohammed and Shirin were waiting. All they could do was hug Hossein and cry. We piled into the back seat of the car. Mohammed whispered to me, "Thanks" and we were off to the house.

We got inside and I put all of the stuff into our bedroom. I turned to look at Hossein and explained that I needed sleep. He understood. Angela went upstairs to play with her cousin while Hossein talked with his family. I think that I slept for about twelve hours. My body said that it had to shut down and recoup. I knew that Hossein needed time with his family. I could hand over the responsibilities to his brother and sister for a while.

The next day, we went to see his cousins that were heart specialists. We needed to get him some oxygen ordered for home and they could do it. They took x-rays of his lungs and we all except Hossein huddled around the pictures. The cousins started to cry and looked at Mohammed. They shook their heads. Everyone understood and they were hugging each other. I could only stand against the wall of the room and silently had tears flowing freely. They all understood what I had been going through and how strong I was to get him back to them.

I did my best to take care of all of Hossein's needs along with taking care of Angela. Shirin helped with the cooking. The cousins were amazed at how Hossein had not lost a lot of weigh which is normal in this situation. I was basically acquiring the tastiest food I could find or make, and feeding him all the time. Of course, I gained weight because of all of this stress. At this point, he stayed on oxygen 24/7.

21
The Drive to Mashhad

We had been back about two weeks. Everyone who was family and friends had visited Hossein. He was not doing well. I had him on morphine from the doctors in Atlanta. It was hard for him to focus. He was in a lot of pain. Any time Angela or any of the other kids in the family got near him, he would ask us to get the kids away so he would not fuss at them. He was dizzy and it was hard for him to focus on things around him. For a day, he did not want any medicine. But sadly, he was in too much pain. He wanted it back after a few hours of not having it.

He told his family that he wanted to go to the Imam Reza Shrine in Mashhad to pray to be healed. They discussed how that could be done. The factory that he had worked for in Kashan arranged an ambulance with a driver to come to our home to take him to Mashhad. We also planned to take Mohammed's small Renault car with us to carry the family.

The drive from Tehran to Mashhad was about 10 hours and 560 miles. We had my husband in the ambulance with his brother. We had his mother, sister, sister-in-law, two kids, and me on the trip in the other car. It was crowded. Of course, in 1988 we did not have safety belts for everyone.

We packed some food for the trip because it was going to be a long drive with very few stops. We were not sure if any food would be available along the way.

On September 7, 1988, a Wednesday, we started the trip. It was our 9th year wedding anniversary. A good day to begin a trip together. The trip seemed very long. Everyone was sad and heart-broken. Their prayers were endless. They wanted Hossein to survive. Prayer was the only answer now.

We had my four-year-old, my sister-in-law's three-year-old, and my five-year-old in the back seat with three ladies. Being already in a small car, they had to sit on our laps. Luckily, we had to entertain them which distracted us from the real reason we were traveling this road. We sang songs, both American and Farsi. Angela had forgotten most of the songs in Farsi and her two cousin did not understand the American ones. So, it kept us busy translating the songs and games for them.

My sister-in-law Ava and I would take turns driving. In Iran, it was legal for women to drive but not very common. Along the way, we were stopped once by police to make sure we were legal. My brother-in-law explained to them what was happening and they let us continue our trip with no problems.

Along the way, we stopped to eat our packed food. Shirin had made some cutlets for us. We were starving. The trip was taking a toll on us all. We were exhausted and one goal was ahead of us. We needed to get to the shrine.

Now it is time to explain a little bit about the shrine and why it was important for Hossein to get there to pray. Think about places people go to get a little extra help in their prayers. For Catholics, it would be the Vatican or one of the many holy sites or churches. For Moslems, it would be Mecca. For Buddhists, it would be the tree that Buda prayed under. Since Hossein could not go to Mecca, Imam Reza's shrine was the best place he could go to in Iran.

An Imam is title for a person who leads prayers in a mosque. Imam Reza was a much respected, knowledgeable, and highly spiritual leader around the year 766 A.D. He was a descendant of the Prophet Muhammad and the eighth Shi'ite Imam. He was poisoned in 818 and buried in a beautiful shrine built for him. Every year in June, millions of Iranians travel to this shrine to attend mourning processions to mark the martyrdom anniversary of Imam Reza. I looked at pictures of the shrine ahead of time. It was beautiful. It was a gold Iranian version of the Taj Mahal in India.

Finally, we got to the shrine in the dusk of the evening. It was crowded. I just followed everyone else because I did not know what to do. I took my daughter's hand and went inside the large courtyard. There were people everywhere camping out on the ground. I could see the gold dome and the minarets on both sides of the dome. It was very awe-inspiring. We found a space in one of the small alcoves to put his stretcher from the ambulance down. We spread out two blankets for everyone to sit near him. The masses of people starred at us. Luckily, no one knew right away that I was foreign.

I do not know if we have courtyards in America like this. I have not been to one here. In Iran, there is an enclosed area like a front yard or a large enclosed courtyard like in New Orleans's French quarter old houses. In this very large area, there are alcoves all around the main square of the courtyard. They are arched and you can be protected from rain or sun. The center of the courtyard normally has a pond or water fountain for the faithful to wash their arms, hands, and feet before prayers.

Large families had gathered in this area to spend the night. The majority were poor and could not afford the cost of a hotel. Many just wanted to stay there to pray and get healed. We were one of the ones needing that healing power. It was very overwhelming to take it all in. I sat next to my husband, trying to get him to eat or drink something. I told him that today was our anniversary and that maybe God would be kind to us. We held hands for a while before he told me and Shirin to go into the mosque portion of the shrine to pray for him. "Yes," I said, "of course."

I followed Shirin into one of the side doors. There were entrances for women and different entrances for men. She led the way through a maze of people and rooms. I could not tell you that I could figure my way back out if I had lost her. I kept my hand on her chador. In a sea of chador coverings, you could easily mistake one lady for another. There was an enclosed fence made of silver and gold. It was very ornate and beautiful. Women were in a line going around on one side of the fence praying and kissing the silver fence. On the other side, men were lined up doing the same thing.

Inside the rectangle fence was a coffin covered with beautiful silk fabric. It looked like money and small pieces of paper with prayers had been placed inside. Monir was praying and kissing the fence and I followed her lead. After a while, we sat down on the carpeted floor and prayed again.

In my heart, I knew that it would certainly be a miracle if Hossein had more time to live.

I told Shirin that I thought we needed to go back to Hossein. I did not want to let Ava have the responsibility to deal with the kids, my mother-in-law, and Hossein too. The men in Iran don't typically entertain children themselves, so Mohammad would not be a lot of help to Eva while she was watching the kids. We needed each other for support. This was a hard thing we had to deal with.

I told Hossein when we got back that I had prayed for him. I told him how much I loved him. He smiled at me and I bend over and gave him a kiss. Our group started to settle in for the night. I told Mohammed that I could not sleep and I would stay up with Hossein. All three of the girls had fallen to sleep. I had alone time with my husband.

It was about 1 a.m. in the early morning. I had been holding his hands. He had been coming in and out of sleep for a while. I talked to him about our future and about having another child in the near future. It made him happy and hopeful. He had fallen asleep and I had cobwebs in my eyes, too. I put my head right next to his arm and closed my eyes.

After a few minutes, he woke me up. He said he needed to urinate. I got a urinal container and cover him with a blanket while he did his best to relieve himself. His breathing was irregular. He was having a lot of trouble breathing even with the oxygen with was bought for his use. I told him that I was going to the bathroom to empty the container and wash up.

After about 10 minutes I came back. Hossein's respiration was slowing down. I thought he was just finally getting some rest, but instead it was his final rest. I checked his vitals, and double-checked to make sure. I woke up his brother. I explained that I believed that Hossein had died. I then let Mohammad check. He got up and went to the small hospital around the corner. I woke all the adults up. He came back with some men and I kiss my husband goodbye. They took him away from the crowd of people watching us. Hossein dies on September 8, 1988, a day after our anniversary. In the Islamic lunar year, it is 1367.

I was crushed. I cried. All of the people around us now knew that I was a foreigner and watched me grieve. I wanted to be alone. I yelled at them to stop looking at me. I was so upset. All I could think of is at least he did not die on our anniversary. We were a group of women who had just lost someone special in our lives; a son, a father, a brother, a brother-in-law, and a husband.

At this point, I had little sleep. I was beyond exhausted. I was a zombie. Angela finally woke up. I took her aside to talk to her. I told her that her dad had been hurting for a while and God came down one of the minarets I pointed to and took him to heaven. I explained how beautiful the minaret was and how her dad would miss her.

By 10 a.m., we had a little sleep. We had a long journey back home to Tehran. Hossein's body was put back into the ambulance. Mohammed rode all the way back with him. I drove a good part of the way. I just followed the back of the ambulance without thinking. I was numb. Ava tried to distract the girls on the long trip back. I had no energy. I had no future to think about at that moment. I just had to get to the next day.

<h1 style="text-align:center">22</h1>

<h1 style="text-align:center">The Funeral</h1>

Thank God for Mohammed. He took care of the details for Hossein. He was put into a morgue in Tehran while we planned his funeral. In Iran, funerals happen fast. They do

not embalm bodies. We had to make some decisions fast. Where would he be buried was the most pressing detail. Mohammed wanted to bury him in Tehran. I wanted him to be buried in Kashan where his friends and extended family lived. It was where we lived. I told Mohammed that he had the final say of course. After talking with the family in Kashan, he decided that there was room in the family mausoleum for him in Kashan.

I remembered that Hossein told me a story about this cemetery in Kashan was one of the seven gates into Heaven. Anyone buried here had an easier time getting to heaven. He thought it was very special. I was glad Mohammed decided to bury him there. Mollamohsen e Faze or another name Akhand e Faze is the name of this cemetery. It is one of the largest cemeteries in Kashan. The cemetery where Hossein is buried is an old one. Hossein used to tell me stories about this place. I knew that this place was where he wanted to be. He loved Kashan.

Hossein was sent ahead of us to be prepared for the burial. He was washed and wrapped in white linen. The box was open with a prayer blanket covering him. We stayed with family members when all of us traveled to Kashan 2 days later. Flyers about the burial were posted everywhere in the city. From what I was told the bazaar and shops were closed for two days for the funeral. Hossein was a member of an old family in the city and a doctor. They wanted to honor him. He was very much loved by the ones who got to know him.

The day of the funeral was a blur to me. I could not have even told you the time of day. All I can remember is that someone in the family took care of Angela and the other kids while the adults went to the funeral. I did not know where to go or what to do. Thank God I had my two sister-in-laws with me. All of the other ladies that attended just followed my lead. Luckily Shirin was there to guide me. There was a man who ordered me and the other women to stay behind the men at all times. While he was giving orders to us, his face was visibly surprised at the foreign woman was leading the group. I said to him in Farsi that I did not understand him. Even in these hard times, there was always a first time for everything. After saying his piece, he politely backed away.

In their culture, they have a funeral procession

that is about a mile long for important people. The men carry their bodies, chant songs, and beat their chests in unison. They had a jeep and someone with a microphone helping to lead the chants. They did this for my husband. He was very much loved by his employees.

In the front of the procession was a man carrying a very wide display of metal signs that waved back and forth as he walked. It is called a Togh and was traditionally used during Imam Hossein's yearly mourning day to honor him on the day he was killed. It was a great honor to have this out in front of an average person. My brother-in-law was very surprised that they were honoring his brother this way. It was usual saved for religious leaders.

Men gathered in the front of the procession behind the sign, and women were relegated to the back. We had to be kept back because of what the men did during the march to the cemetery. They carried the body but others wanted the honor to carry the body too. It was a little confusing to watch different guys trying to carry the body without dropping him.

It was a pulsating mass of men holding him beautifully. The chanting sounds that the men made along the way were mesmerizing. The beat drove me forward. I could not feel myself walking. Hundreds of people were in step with us and others were standing on the sides of the road. This was a large funeral and I was not expecting all of this. I felt at home with these people. A lot of them were my friends and cared about me. They were honoring me, too. I brought him home to die with his family and friends. They knew I loved him.

When we got to the cemetery, the men went inside the mausoleum with his body.  My brother-in-law requested a photographer from the carpet factory to take pictures for me of the funeral. I could not witness firsthand the burial itself, but the photos helped me understand later what had happened. They carried him in and took him out of the wooden box. He was wrapped up in linen. They removed the stone slab from the floor, and one of his cousins dropped into the small vault that could contain 2 bodies. They have the mausoleum set up with  concrete boxes under the floor for burials. With help from others, his cousin lowered him down into the crypt box and replaced the concrete slab on top of

the floor. He was buried on September 16th, 1988. I wrote in my small journal about this date. It is the date every year, we were to return to the gravesite to honor him. I would have to let my sister-in-law Shirin keep this tradition alive for him in the future.

The men of the family gathered in the room to cry and talk about Hossein while we waited outside. Eventually, they left and we women were allowed to go in. I sat down on the floor near my husband's grave with Shirin and cried. It was done. He was finally at rest. He was not in pain anymore. I could collapse. My body was in a state of exhaustion. I had done so much in these past weeks. I was so happy for all of the support of Hossein's family and friends.

Just like we have wakes at home in the states, they have similar traditions, too. Somebody ordered a ton of food, and a large amount of family and friends came to our house. If I remember correctly, we were in my sister-in-law Ava's

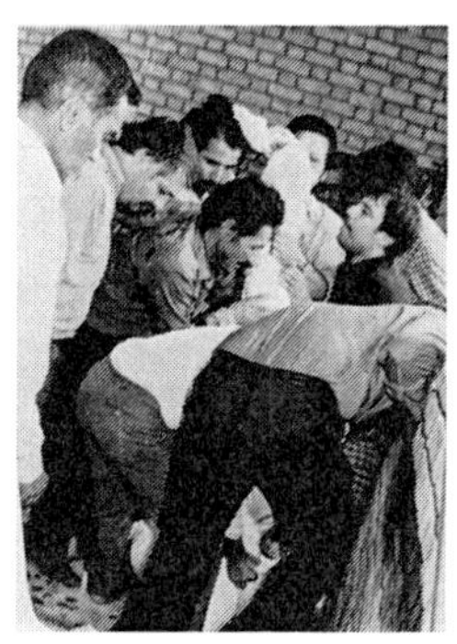

brother's home. I could not last the evening. My head was hurting from a very bad migraine. I let my brother-in-law take charge of greeting the people. This continued for two days. I was able to attend on the second day once my headache subsided. I heard a poet read a poem that was written for Hossein. We sat all around the rooms against the walls and listened to people talk and say prayers.

It is tradition to have three days of mourning, then 7 days later, an additional mourning day. We had these events but my mind was blank as to what had happened. Later, we drove back to Tehran. We all crashed and took some time to recuperate. The family explained to me that there would be a 40-day ceremony and a one-year ceremony at Hossein's gravesite. I said that I would stay in Iran for 40 days but I needed to go back to America with Angela before the year was up.

Mohammed had already spent a lot of money on the funeral and all of the details. I called my dad and asked him to pay for an airplane ticket for Angela and me to come back home. I would  pay him back later. So, for the next few weeks, I visited family members to say our goodbyes. I went with Shirin to the bazaar in Tehran and bought some special materials. It was to be made into a small tablecloth to be put on top of Hossein's tomb. In Iran, it was believed that poor people were closer to god, so it became the norm to place sweets on top a tablecloth on graves, to ask for prayers from the less fortunate. Shirin helped me to make halwa (a confectionary paste similar to peanut butter, without the peanuts) to be put into little sweet sandwiches. We also packed fruit and cucumbers. I was not sure when we would be able to come back. Angela got reintroduced to the language, but English was her mainstay for comfort. She could not understand much of what was happening around her except that her dad was not there.

We finally traveled to Kashan for the last time before leaving. Shirin showed me how the sweets and other foods we made needed to be placed on the tablecloth. It was available to the people who would visit the gravesite to show their respects. We also had purchased some prayer tapes to play on a cassette recorder. We sat down on the carpet and laid that special fabric down on top of the grave. Shirin placed the fruits and sweets we made on the cover. We had people visiting the site for hours. A lot of the visitors were poor, we gave them food and they offered their prayers.

Our plane tickets were scheduled for the very next week. I left the things that I had brought with me four years ago to my two sisters-in-law. Angela and I each left with one suitcase. We had a layover in London of about fourteen hours. I wanted to go into the city but I wanted to make sure we made it home with some cash in my pocket. We had to switch airports in London and we just hung around the terminal until our flight home. When we touched down in Atlanta, I felt that about ten years had passed by instead of just four. Time to rethink my life and my daughter's future.

A tradition of wearing black…

In many older traditions, women wore black for a least a year after a close member of their family dies. I did my best to honor Hossein with this tradition. Even today, my wardrobe is about 75% black. One of my friends told me that I wear so many shades of black.

This is a poem from local Iranian poet.

In memory of the late Dr. Hossein Atrchin.

You befriended us and were a loyal friend for a while.

What did we do that you didn't like and made you leave us?

My moon! Your love grew in from the bosoms of springtime. 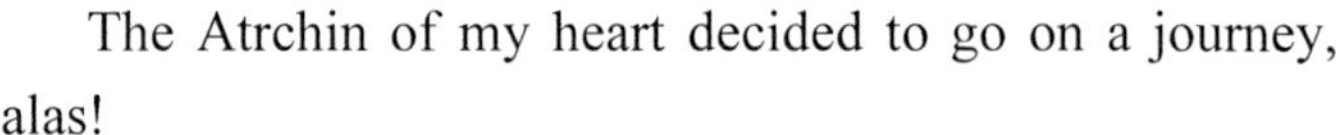

And you turned into a flower, emotion, mirror, and meadow!

Yesternight I was telling myself in the mirror of my tears.

How miserably I am enchained to the sorrow of separation!

The Atrchin of my heart decided to go on a journey, alas!

I want all flowers to go as without him they are turned into thorns.

Oh Saem, this ghazal is your way to my farewell.

To that gazelle who was such a loyal friend!

23

The Return

When Angela and I got back to America we stayed with my father for a while. We had to recuperate from my husband's death. We moved on with our lives. I was able to keep in communication with my husband's family. We sent some presents for the now two daughters of Mohammed and talked together on the phone on holidays. Hossein's mother passed away about a year after Hossein had died. Mohammed had a new apartment house he had built and was living in with his  family. They were doing fairly well. The war had ended the year after Hossein had died so I was not worried about that problem.

Almost 13 years later, Angela was almost seventeen years old. She had experienced some American prejudice being half Iranian. One of her neighborhood friend's parents had even called her several slurs once he discovered her heritage. It was sad that even after 10 years, ignorant people were still around. I had a deep sadness about American perceptions of Iran.

I wanted Angela to see Iran for herself. I did not want her to be indoctrinated by American propaganda regarding the culture or people there. I wanted her to visit her family in Iran before she got too independent and off to college. I started to plan our trip there. We had to go on Iranian passports into the county. No Americans were allowed except under special conditions. The Pakistan Iranian-interest section was able to get our old passports updated. It took about two months to get our documents in order.

I got on the phone in early February with Mohammed to work out the details. I brought our tickets for the middle of August a two-week trip. We would be back in time for Angela's school to start. We were all excited.

A couple of weeks later, my sister-in-law Ava called. Mohammad had been meeting with some men in his home office. He started to feel weak, fell, and had a deadly heart attack. I was in shock. I had just made plans with him to see Angela after so many years and now he was dead. I said my apologies to Ava. She said she would understand if we canceled our trip. No, we were still coming. I told her I wanted to visit his grave at the very least and honor him. I was very sad that Angela would not be able to be reintroduced to her only uncle.

So, on August 15th, 2001 we got on a plane with a layover in Amsterdam, Netherlands. I had made long coats and scarves for us to wear when we got on the final leg of our trip to Iran. We had presents for everyone that we could remember. There was a young boy cousin that we had not met yet. Even though it was sad not to have Mohammad there, the rest of the family would be reunited with Angela.

In Amsterdam, we had a ten-hour layover. I wanted to get into the city and explore it before we left. I had done some research before we got there. It was an easy 20-minute train ride from the airport to the city center. Our luggage was thankfully being transferred to the new airplane for us, so we did not have to deal with our heavy suitcases while touring Amsterdam. We got to the main terminal and discussed our plans. I knew that I wanted to ride a boat on the canals and walk around for a bit. I let Angela decide on two other things we could do. This was her trip, too. I wanted her have her say, and take ownership of a part of the itinerary.

We had looked through the Amsterdam brochure on what visitors could do in a day. She read it carefully and decided that visiting Anne Frank's house and going to the Sex Museum was at the top of her list. Well, I did not have a problem with Anne Frank, but there were so many better museums to see instead. The Van Gogh Museum and Rijksmuseum were renowned for their exhibits. She was not interested. She was not interested so I broke down and we went to these two places. The Frank exhibit was great and the Sex Museum was not too bad, either. I guess that we would not forget our experience in Amsterdam.

We got back to the airport with plenty of time to spare. We put on our coats and scarves for the next leg of our adventure. This was a new feeling for Angela. The last time she was in Iran was when she was four. She did not know the language except for a few words. We checked through customs with no problem. They knew that we were foreigners but I could speak Farsi with no problem. I did have my American passports with me concealed in a zipped-up part of my purse. I did not have it out in plain sight but I did not want to act like I was smuggling it in.

Ava was waiting for us with her three kids. She greeted us and we collected the luggage. We drove to her new house in the northern part of Tehran called Shemrom. Since it was only two weeks and I wanted Angela to see as much of the area as possible while we were there, we planned out our stay very carefully. For the first four days, we would visit Shirin, family, and friends in Tehran and Kashan. And for a week we would travel with Ava and her kids to Isfahan and Shiraz. For the last two days, we would be back with Shirin and would get back on the plane going home.

We handled out our gifts to everyone, had some pizza, and then talked and played music. It was a very nice treat for Angela and me. She didn't remember the songs and the way Ava could drum. It was very soothing. We talked about the things that happened when the kids were young. For example, Ava loved to pinch Angela's cheeks on her face until she was crying. She considered it an act of love. One-time Angela's oldest cousin was playing with her outside and she came back inside crying. I tried to ask her what happened. She simply kept crying until I noticed a round bruise on her forehead. Somehow her cousin had bitten her there and I could not understand how she did it. Ava was red from embarrassment that her daughter had done that. I explained to Ava that these things happen, and not to worry about it. Angela and her cousin were always getting into trouble. I loved it.

The next day we got a taxi to Shirin's new home farther north in Tehran. She had an apartment to herself since she had retired. She spoke very little English but we began where we left off years ago. It seemed like it was just yesterday. Angela started to pick up some words between Shirin and me teaching her.

The next day we left by bus to Kashan. We had a lot of family and places to visit. We stayed with one of Hossein's cousins for the days we were there. She took us to a village where she had a garden home. Neighbors came to greet us and Angela got to experience an Iranian ladies' tea party. They sat, drank tea, and sang. It was so calming. When the ladies left, Angela and I got to get into a small pond that had spring water feeding it. Being so hot, the water was so cold. Angela fell in love with this garden and pond.

The next day we traveled all around Kashan. We visited our old house, and the street we lived on. We went to the Fin Garden. We dipped our feet into the cold water at center while we enjoyed the view. It has very tall cypress trees throughout the garden with fountains everywhere. Afterward, we drove along Finn street and had some kabab. We sat cross-legged on special carpeted raised platforms with pillows behind us. Think of a very short wooden table, covered in Persian carpet. We were right next to a little spring that traveled beside the street, and it was serene.

Kashan is a very hot place during the summer. I was trying to make memories for Angela but it was so hot. We were covered head to toe in dark clothing and sauntered along the dusty street looking for shadows to stand in away from the heat. In some of the back alleys, we found a hookah place. It had benches for people to sit in the shade of some trees. We crashed. Someone there had a hookah and showed her how to smoke it. I think that she was having fun.

The day before we left, we visited Hossein's grave. Before his death, Mohammad had gotten a grave marker that was beautiful. It was engraved in gold on white marble. At the bottom of the marker, it said in English, "To our beloved husband and father." Mohammed wanted us to feel a part of the family who loved Hossein. I wished that I could have hugged him at this moment. That was so special.

We got back to Tehran and joined Ava and her kids for the next leg of our journey. She paid for all of our travel expenses. I told her not to, but she said that Mohammad would want it that way. I thanked her so much for her kindness. So we have Angela who was 17, her cousins (ages 18, 16, 11), Ava, and myself on this expedition of what Iran had to offer. For our first destination, we traveled by train from Tehran to Isfahan. We stayed in a hotel right next to the main Shah's square. We visited all of the sites that we had done so many years ago when Angela barely 1-year-old. Angela and her cousins were having a great time. They would tease each other without speaking much English or Farsi. I think that her cousins were enjoying being taught English by her and vice versa.

I was so happy that she was able to see these places that her dad and I had gone to. The next stop on our trip was by Iran Air into Shiraz. One of the places we stopped by to visit was the Nasir al-Mulk Mosque (nicknamed the pink mosque). It is famous for its stained-glass windows. You can sit down on the floor and watch the kaleidoscopic color play on the ground. The sun and clouds move around in the sky to create amazing patterns. I pointed out the pixelated Kufi script from the Koran on the walls of the different mosques we travelled through. The writing is so mesmerizing, it was hard to understand that it was Arabic script.

Shiraz is where we got to see Persepolis, temples, and a fire temple. Standing in the shadow of these monumental buildings, it felt like she got to glimpse into the past and marvel at the ancient cultures, customs, and religions. Of course, we had to visit the royal capital of Pasargadae and King Cyrus's grave. We stopped along the way to visit a roadside stand to get some fruit. Angela wanted to take some pictures of herself with her cousins and the young boys selling the fruit. We looked at the scenic farmland around us. The mountains surrounded the land which made it such a unique spot.

We finally left on the overnight train back to Tehran. It felt like a country wide tour. We got to see so many things in so little time. Ava was so attentive to our wants and needs. She wanted Angela to have the best memories. We visited Freedom Tower near the airport one more time. We visited my mother-in-law and Mohammad's grave. We gave our prayers of remembrance to them. We visited Shirin one more time and had dinner with other family members. They gave us gifts of saffron, sweets, and a beautiful small handmade rug for Angela. It was hard to say goodbye. I was very glad that Angela and I was having some closure on visiting Iran and the family that we had grown to love. She had gotten to know them. Good memories are important to make.

Angela and I make the most of this trip. So much was accomplished in these two weeks. Again, we had no trouble getting out of the county. My father would say that I could get shit on my shoes, and get into a mess, but I would come out smelling like a rose. Two weeks later, 9/11 happened. Life turned upside down and planes were not going anywhere. Timing is sometimes everything. We had made it home.

24

The Time of This Writing

I retired from teaching public school at the beginning of the summer of 2019. I did a little substituting and committing myself to write this part of my life. There were too many friends who had heard bits and pieces of my story and insisted that I needed to share it. I goofed off for a while not focusing on the book until Covid-19 appeared on the horizon. It made me get going. I am older now and have some health issues. I hoped that you have found my story interesting. It is as true as I can remember to the best of my ability. My book's title "Just Add Rosewater", is a true allegory of my life. Just like my father comparing me to roses, my husband's family business of selling rosewater, and the taste of roses added to almost every dish, I felt like my life was infused with roses. Once I came back to America, I felt like my life had been diluted. Now every time I come across something that reminds me of a rose, I feel like it reenergizes me with a bittersweet melancholy. All of the pictures are mine and I hoped that seeing them helps you travel on my journey, too. I never claimed to be a great writer, but none the less, I had a story to tell.

Shab behesht (Good heaven)
and
Shab bekheir (Good night)